Managing Projects at Work

For Anne, Claire and Lorna
from a grateful husband and Daddy.

Managing Projects at Work

Gordon Webster

Gower

Published by
Gower Publishing Limited
Gower House
Croft Road
Aldershot
Hampshire GU11 3HR
England

Gower
Old Post Road
Brookfield
Vermont 05036
USA

British Library Cataloguing in Publication Data
Webster, Gordon
    Managing projects at work
    1. Industrial project management
    I. Title
    658.4'04

ISBN 0 566 07982 8

Typeset in 10/12 Sabon by Wearset, Boldon, Tyne and Wear
Printed in Great Britain at the University Press, Cambridge

Contents

List of figures   vii

Acknowledgements   xi

Introduction   1

PART I   BUILDING THE DEFENSIBLE PLAN   11

CHAPTER 1   The Defensible Plan   13

CHAPTER 2   Defining your project   17

CHAPTER 3   Scheduling the work   27

CHAPTER 4   Estimating resources needed   43

CHAPTER 5   Planning for project leadership   53

CHAPTER 6   Managing risk   73

CHAPTER 7   Delighting customers   81

CHAPTER 8   Building a budget   97

CHAPTER 9   Selling the Defensible Plan   107

PART II   IMPLEMENTING THE DEFENSIBLE
              PLAN   115

CHAPTER 10   Project implementation, an overview   117

CHAPTER 11   Building and using project controls   125

CHAPTER 12   Leading and motivating project team members   147

CHAPTER 13   Building and leading a project team   165

CHAPTER 14   Solving implementation problems   181

Glossary   191

Index   193

List of figures

I.1	The two parts of a manager's job	4
I.2	Matrix working	5
I.3	The operational cycle	6
I.4	Project life cycle	7
I.5	The Defensible Plan	8
2.1	Project context	20
2.2	Task and process	22
2.3	Roles	22
2.4	The sequence to produce a project definition	23
2.5	An example of a project definition	24
3.1	Shopping list	28
3.2	Shopping list breakdown	29
3.3	Establish the right order for visiting	30
3.4	Project functions	31
3.5	Project plan	31
3.6	Add names to your network chart	32
3.7	Activity description sheet	33
3.8	Activity data summary	34
3.9	Project network diagram	36
3.10	Add duration times	37
3.11	Forward pass calculation	37
3.12	Backward pass (as bold arrow)	38
3.13	Fixing a future date (as bold arrow)	39
3.14	Calculating slack or float	40
3.15	Critical path	41
4.1	Add the number of people needed	44
4.2	From network to bar chart	46
4.3	Resource profile	47
4.4	Reducing the manning peak	47
4.5	Level resources plan	48
4.6	Using total slack	50
4.7	Simple subtraction exercise	50
5.1	The three circles of need	54
5.2	Distortion of circles caused by over emphasis on one activity	55
5.3	Project team working	57

5.4	The standing project team	59
5.5	Implementation plan—outline format	60
5.6	Key competencies	62
5.7	Team competencies table	63
5.8	Implementation plan—competencies added	64
5.9	Implementation plan—tasks added	66
5.10	The implementation cycle	67
5.11	Implementation plan—training and meetings added	71
6.1	Impact/probability matrix	76
6.2	Updated impact/probability matrix	78
7.1	Components of a quality plan: the parts	83
7.2	Satisfaction levels	88
7.3	Enhancements	91
7.4	Quality reviews	92
7.5	Implementation plan: task, project and supplier reviews added	94
8.1	Implementation plan updated	100
8.2	Budget summary—task and quality hours	101
8.3	Budget summary	103
9.1	Project presentation—proposed structure, content and timing	111
10.1	The three spheres	118
10.2	Work breakdown of an implementation plan	118
10.3	Herrmann thinking styles: four quadrants, labelled anticlockwise A–D	119
10.4	Project management activity applying Herrmann's metaphor	120
10.5	Additions to Herrmann	122
10.6	Effective decisions are 'whole brained'	123
11.1	Instrument panel	127
11.2	Changes observed	127
11.3	Project performance	130
11.4	Staff utilisation	131
11.5	Task hours and percentage complete	132
11.6	Task hours and completion table	133
11.7	Forecast final hours	134
11.8	Base line forecast hours	134
11.9	Customer satisfaction	135
11.10	Project status table	137
11.11	Task hours and percentage complete (week 3)	138
11.12	Project performance (week 3)	139
11.13	Staff utilisation	140
11.14	Forecast final hours	141
11.15	Customer satisfaction (week 3)	141
11.16	Status forecast for end of week 5	143
11.17	Task hours and percentage complete (forecast week 5)	143

11.18	What if?—status forecast for end of week 5	144
11.19	Task hours and percentage complete (What if?— forecast week 5)	145
12.1	Power and influence	148
12.2	One structure	151
12.3	Matching power, leadership style and maturity	153
12.4	Leadership style and the project life cycle	154
12.5	Motivation balance	155
12.6	Job context	156
12.7	Context and content of the job	157
12.8	Five levels of disclosure	159
12.9	Transition curve	161
13.1	Briefing model	175
13.2	Life cycle of a project	177
13.3	Beginning the project implementation cycle	178
13.4	Middle of the project implementation cycle	179
13.5	End of the project implementation cycle	179
14.1	Task hours and percentage complete (week 3)	182
14.2	Staff utilisation (week 3)	183
14.3	Project performance (week 3)	184
14.4	Project implementation: example of Herrmann	185
14.5	Performance fishbone	186
14.6	Performance and people factors	187
14.7	Staff utilisation	187
14.8	Questionnaire	189

Acknowledgements

Thanks to:

- Friend and colleague Gavin Barrett of PA Consulting Group, who convinced me that I had something to say to the world of management and who cajoled and pushed me to write this book.
- Those at PA/Sundridge Park with whom I worked over the past decade developing ideas and applying them in successful practice.
- The many clients with whom I work for taking the risks in adopting the methods taught in these pages.
- Ron Cox and Tim Andrews of Management Worlds Inc. of Summit, New Jersey, USA for their help in providing examples and models.
- Ned Herrmann, John Adair, Carole Pemberton, Ken Blanchard, Meredith Belbin, Rupert Eales-White and other management writers for their frameworks and concepts which helped when illustrating project management thinking.

A very special thanks to friend and business partner Tony Paris whose ideas and experiences from over 20 years of developing the methods contained here, provided much of the structure and content of this book.

G.W.

Introduction

This is a 'how to' book for anyone who manages projects in addition to their daily duties. More and more managers, of all disciplines, in today's business environment find themselves both managing and working on projects—as well as carrying out their usual activities. This book shows managers how to go about planning and delivering a project in a series of structured steps. It assumes no prior knowledge and it does not go further into the subject of project management than is necessary for the delivery of a single project; that is, one involving a number of people from either the same or different parts of an organisation. The book puts the essential fundamentals in place which in themselves are complex enough for the majority of projects at work. Most of the lessons taught here are a direct result of working with professional project managers over many years.

So, what do we mean by projects at work? Let's look at two examples.

John was upset. As an area sales manager he felt he had enough on his hands without being asked to do additional work—the launch of a new product his sales director had asked him to introduce to the sales force. Of course, with the downsizing that had taken place over recent years there was no longer any marketing support; if the sales force needed brochures they would just have to do the work themselves. John had drawn the short straw. It was an honour to be asked, of course, but he still had his sales work to do. Somehow he just had to fit everything into the time available. But working time would eat into his personal life—again. His last *ad hoc* project—introducing the new sales control software to the sales force—was supposed to be a little additional task that would take 'only a few hours'. It ended up taking weeks as it became clear that he was the only person who understood both the old and the new system. This resulted in much travelling, as he made a presentation for every field sales manager throughout the country. No-one had foreseen that happening and the sales on his territory suffered as a result.

Susan wasn't much happier than John. She had a training department to run for a highly technical organisation. Now she had been asked to organise the annual dealer conference for 500 people. As dealer support operated from the field there was no-one at head office to coordinate all the activities. In addition, there was no-one to help her with the vital technical training work. But somehow everything had to get done. There goes her weekend—again. Her last *ad hoc* project had been to make recommendations for the layout and equipment of a new training facility: 'Susan's in the business so it shouldn't take more than a few hours.' No-one had said anything about briefing architects, contractors and the builders; or anticipated the many meetings that were needed to ensure that her recommendations were practical for the shape and size of the facility being built.

John and Susan are typical of managers in today's organisations. They have their own work and they have additional work. The additional work is taking up more and more of their available time.

In recent times it has become noticeable that in increasing numbers managers like John and Susan are not fully enjoying their work. Many have experienced recession but there is more to this malaise than difficult market conditions. In the safe confines of an external training environment many managers talk increasingly about:

- increasing volumes of work;
- longer and longer working hours just to keep up with the volume;
- feelings of frustration as the bottom of the work pile is seldom reached;
- difficulty in getting access or support from their bosses;
- shortage of resources and the pressure to keep staff levels low;
- increasing market competition with profit margins eroding.

Managers feel that they are no longer in control of their working lives; their home relationships are suffering and they have little time for anything other than work. They worry about the future knowing that the way they work is not sustainable or indeed desirable. So many people not enjoying their working lives clearly indicates that all is not well in the management world.

A new way of working

John and Susan are being asked to work in a new way and much of their discontent stems from not understanding this. Today, hierarchies with many layers of management between customer and chief executive can no longer be paid for, so organisations are leaner and slimmer and more has to be done by fewer people. These new 'flat' organisations have little 'slack' or spare capacity to get essential additional tasks done. When downsizing is planned, the focus of the planners is on the core operations—the key activities of the business. What is the minimal number of people needed to deliver this core product? Following this downsizing, typically, there is just enough capacity to deliver the operational needs of the business with nothing left over for anything else. So when it comes to updating the IT system or launching a new product, or producing a contingency plan for an unwanted event, there is no-one left to do it—except for operational managers. Two more examples explore this trend.

A client of mine was anticipating a strike by field engineers as a result of a breakdown in negotiations with national unions. He worked for an elevator company and, as public safety was at stake, a manager with a fully operational role was required as a National Strike Coordinator. My client undertook this task, in a company which had been downsized and was operating a pretty tight ship as far as resources were concerned. He was asked to produce a plan that, in the event of a strike, would swing into action to provide essential services using non-union managers and administrators to cover safety requirements. With many thousands of elevators to be kept operational this was a huge task. My client achieved it without any reduction in his operational duties.

In my last job, I had an operational role in developing and delivering programmes to bring about organisational change for clients. Although enjoyable it was hard work with long hours often spent overseas. Like most managers, by Friday or Saturday my energy levels were low. Yet, along with my colleagues, I was continually working on additional tasks. I was chairing a project to improve internal communications. A colleague was asked to make recommendations about the handling of our key accounts. Another had to research and make recommendations covering the use of IT in the lecture room. There was no question of laying off operational responsibility to get these additional tasks done. They were a part of the job although they did not appear as such on our job descriptions. It was unusual to have only one additional task running at any one time, it was more likely to be two or three each.

This *modus operandi* reflects the new ways that managers must now adopt. Reputations are more likely to be built on the delivery of *ad hoc* projects than in operational jobs. These projects are often highly visible across many departments and success or otherwise can be crucial for careers.

Jobs in two parts

In this new climate, the job of the manager has two separate parts: there is operational (or functional) work and there is project work. The proportions may differ from job to job but the two parts will be there in most work the manager undertakes.

The diagonal arrows in Figure I.1 represent the impact that each part of the job has on the other part. The day to day work has to be done

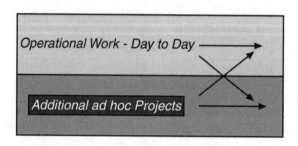

Figure I.1   The two parts of a manager's job

but projects interfere with this process and the day to day work prevents full concentration on the projects. Managing day to day operational work is an ongoing process and it is often repetitive, involving more of the same as the week before. Problems have to be solved but the operational aspects of work roll on and on. Projects are different. They are finite, having to be delivered in a given period of time. They have a clear beginning and an end. They may involve people that we do not usually work with and we may not have any formal authority over them. They are not repeated and they could have a discrete budget to get the work done.

If you do not recognise these *ad hoc* projects in your own work, projects will exist in other forms. For example, a sales manager is operational most of the time but when a request to tender for new business arrives it can represent days of work with inputs needed from many other departments. The sales manager is now leading a project as well as a sales team. Similarly, a service manager despatching engineers to maintain equipment is running an operation until the day when a major repair is required, then he or she too becomes a project manager. In the business environment of today most managers are project managers.

These projects need numbers of people, they are too big to be done alone by the manager in charge. In many cases no-one is allocated to help. It is the job of the manager to find help—that's a part of the project. My client, the National Strike Coordinator, led a project team of 17 people from various parts of the country, all recruited by him as volunteers to help. Whether people are allocated or not, the project manager will end up managing a project with people from a number of disciplines who need to be led to complete the work on time.

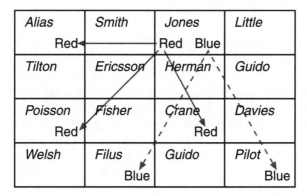

Figure I.2   Matrix working

Matrix working

When managing projects, the environment in which a manager works is a matrix—not the hierarchy in which he or she delivers the operational part of the job. The triangular hierarchy is familiar: each employee sits somewhere in the triangle reporting to a boss higher up the triangle. In a matrix, each employee occupies his or her own 'box' and relates to other workers in other boxes. When delivering projects, some boxes (people) will get together to work on a project, but the following day those boxes will be working with different boxes on another project. In Figure I.2, Jones is working on project Red and Blue. The people she is working with on project Red are not the same as those on project Blue.

Project Blue is a project to change the company paper invoice so that it is more 'customer friendly'. Jones from accounts is the project manager and she has persuaded Pilot from marketing and Filus from customer services to help her. She is also the project manager for Project Red, a project introducing a new software package to the accounts department. Here she has been given Poisson and Crane from the IT department and she has asked Alias from sales to help—Alias was a member of a project team that recently set-up a computerised sales system. The team experienced problems and Jones would like to use their experience to avoid similar problems on Project Red.

In today's organisations we can be working in a hierarchy for our ongoing operational work and in a matrix for the additional *ad hoc* tasks or projects we are asked to carry out, alongside our operational duties. To a large extent, in hierarchies staff are looked after by the boss. Work is allocated from above and the boss has a good picture of who is doing what. In matrices the individual is more responsible for what they take on.

In a matrix environment people come together to carry out a specific task and disband when it is finished. Team members then move onto new projects, probably staffed by a different team of people.

The matrix is much more loose and informal meaning that there is no 'central registry' of who is doing what on which project. Staff have more responsibility for looking after themselves. How many of us actually know what our working capacity is? We know when we have too much or too little but few of us can actually quantify it.

So, when we are asked to do an additional piece of work we have little idea how much spare capacity we have to respond with. On top of that the task will not have been defined in terms of the amount of effort required. We then have the double whammy of being asked to do something—but nobody knows exactly how much, combined with little knowledge about whether or not there are resources available to do the something. It is little wonder that managers are frustrated.

Operational versus project working

Operational management and project management are by nature different and therefore need different skills.

Operations (Figure I.3) are about continuity—more or less of the same. On the other hand, projects (Figure I.4) are linear. They have a defined start point and a defined finish point. They have a beginning, a middle, and an end with activity generally peaking in the middle.

Projects are unique, finite and temporary. They bring people together who may work with each other only on this project. They encourage matrix working. For example, producing a product brochure will need expertise in marketing, copy writing, photography, graphics, legal aspects, technical matters, printing and distribution. Such expertise may be provided by people who do not work in the same department or it could be sourced from outside the organisation.

Operations

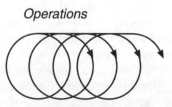

Figure I.3   The operational cycle

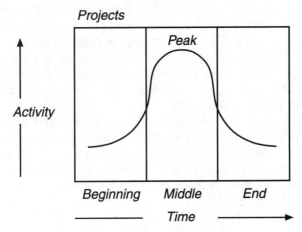

Figure I.4   Project life cycle

Most managers are trained to run their operations either formally or through gaining experience as they make their way up the promotion ladder. They are unlikely to have been trained in project management. So they are running projects as a part of their operation instead of managing them as projects. By force-fitting their projects in with the operation means that they are also forced to react to project needs as they occur. Hence the unexpected and unwanted long hours on projects and the frustration and resentment that ultimately comes with it. As things stand there is no reason why this situation should change. Unquantified tasks are constantly being given out to managers who immediately start implementing them, without enough thought being given to the resources needed and where they are to come from. Only about one third of the way into the project is the size of the task understood and a mad scramble then starts to try to complete on time without adequate resources.

Poor project management generates wasted effort, frustration and discontent. Today's manager needs the knowledge, behaviour and competence of a project manager as part of his or her personal effectiveness toolkit.

Why read this book?

If you read this book and apply the methods it recommends you will be a better manager. You will be more in control of your working life and therefore less stressed and frustrated. You will have a thorough working knowledge of the basic tools of the project manager but, more importantly, you will know how they should be used. You will also be aware of their limitations and the traps and pitfalls waiting for the inexperienced or unwary. The common sense applied leadership techniques introduced in the planning stage and taken through to implementation can be used effectively in any situation where people work together. Mastering these techniques will enhance your operational leadership as well as your project management.

You will learn how to plan and organise a project and how to deliver it successfully through good leadership, combined with the appropriate use of effective project management tools. You will be able to respond professionally to *ad hoc* project requests, presenting yourself as a capable and competent manager who knows how to be effective in the business environment of today.

The structure of this book

The book is in two parts. Part One, 'Building the Defensible Plan', will teach you how to create a project plan. This Defensible Plan is the cornerstone of any project as it shapes and determines everything that follows; it is made of eight sections (Figure I.5). Each of these sections is discussed in detail in this first part.

In Part Two of the book, 'Implementing the Defensible Plan', the key lessons of project implementation and delivery are addressed.

A glossary of project management terms may be found at the end of the book, just before the Index.

Figure I.5   The Defensible Plan

Chapter 1 is an overview of what we have to do to gain control of a project, thereby reducing stress on ourselves and others. Here the Defensible Plan is introduced—arguably the greatest stress reducer for any overworked manager.

Chapter 2 defines the work we are asked to do. Are we absolutely clear *why* this work is needed and *what* needs to be done?

Chapter 3 uses the tools of project management to make visible our work so that we can schedule with some degree of accuracy. Here we are addressing *how* work can be done.

Having assessed how long the work will take, we can estimate the resources we will need to help us achieve the objective; we will do this in Chapter 4.

Chapter 5 introduces project leadership and the necessity to write plans that will accommodate the needs of the project and those of the people carrying it out.

Consideration of risk and associated insurances is discussed in Chapter 6 and the delivering of customer delight through quality in Chapter 7.

The cost of the work we want to do is assessed in Chapter 8; the case for the Defensible Plan is presented in Chapter 9.

To end Part One, and the planning phase having achieved agreement for our plan, we look to implementation and decide how we are going to *control* the work when it starts, ensuring that we know what is happening now and in the future. Having first looked at an overall view of implementation in Chapter 10 we will fully complete the Defensible Plan by defining key project success factors and how they can be measured and controlled so as to keep projects on track.

Chapter 11 addresses the interpretation of these controls and how they can best be used.

Chapter 12 is more specific about the leadership and motivation of individuals engaged in projects.

In Chapter 13, the growth and development of project teams is examined.

Finally, Chapter 14 deals with problem solving on projects at work.

Part I
Building the
Defensible Plan

The Defensible Plan

Plans are the tangible evidence of the thinking of managers.
J. O. McKinsey

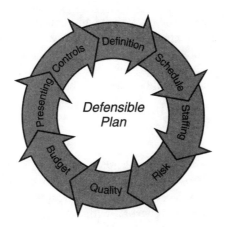

McKinsey tells us to look at a plan to see the management thinking behind it. He is also telling us that the very existence of a plan indicates that some thinking must have taken place. In our management lives plans are not always written down but with projects only the smallest tasks do not have a written plan. The production of a plan requires the application of reasoning and logic to ensure that others understand what should happen according to the plan. A plan is a form of communication that ensures that all concerned are 'singing from the same song sheet'—the plan is the song sheet.

The structure of the Defensible Plan

The Defensible Plan is so called because when correctly built it can be presented confidently and then defended. The process involved in its production covers all aspects of a project. Each part of the plan leads logically to the next until it is complete. It results in a plan which is thorough, justifiable, workable and visible. This approach has been developed over a 20-year period and is used as the preferred method of many leading organisations from a number of industry sectors in many parts of the world. It consists of eight distinct but overlapping steps.

1. Defining the project
2. Scheduling the work
3. Estimating and allocating resources
4. Managing risk
5. Delivering quality
6. Building a budget
7. Selling the plan
8. Setting up controls

If all of these steps are in the plan, the planning is sound. If one of the steps is missing it is unlikely to be a Defensible Plan. It follows a logical planning flow with each step following on in sequence from the previous. If a step is missed out the following steps cannot be done fully and the result is an indefensible plan, as there will be questions that cannot be answered.

Why plan?

On being given an additional task, the temptation is to get on with it as soon as possible. There is already too much work and not enough time so there is pressure to do everything quickly, and to implement as soon as possible. There is nothing wrong with getting off to a flying start provided we start at the right place. The right place is the beginning and the beginning is the plan.

The plan defines the role of the project manager and allocates responsibilities and roles to those involved in the project's delivery. Planning brings out options for actions which allows choice and proactivity, rather than reaction to circumstances as they occur. The process allows for planned coordination of effort which reduces the amount of resources needed. When projects are delivered by crisis management they will use more resources as people are taken on to catch up and then let go until the next crisis.

For all the above reasons, planning reduces stress on the manager. As a result of producing a plan he or she will have a good mental picture of the whole task and where and how it should be at any given point of time.

What happens if there is no plan?

Without a plan it is easy to work very hard to end up in a different place from the desired end. Poor planning produces:

- confusion
- lack of common understanding

- higher costs
- stress and discontent
- missed deadlines
- lack of resource
- duplication of effort
- rework.

Ultimately disaster happens. There are many cliches to support this thinking. 'Failing to plan is planning to fail' and the 5 P's: *Poor Planning Produces Pathetic Performance* and so on. If planning is so important why is it avoided?

Why is planning avoided?

There are many reasons for not planning, most of them emotional:

- Planning is a mentally demanding exercise, it hurts!
- Planning is a 'self starting' process, it needs an effort of will to get it going.
- Planning is not reactive, it needs decisions to be made about what will happen in advance. In our busy working lives we can become skilled at reacting to circumstances rather than creating them: 'I'm good at fire fighting so I enjoy having fires to put out.'
- It takes courage to publicly commit to a specific course of action; when plans are written personal risk is involved because at some stage commitment to that plan will be needed.
- 'Projects are never delivered to plan so what's the point?' The production of the plan brings intimate knowledge of the project. When the plan needs to flex (as it must) this in-depth knowledge gives a better chance of the correct action.
- Planning is boring. It is for most people but project planning can be interesting.

Making planning interesting

Planning is seen as dry and dusty but project planning is 'planning for real'. It is not some remote strategic exercise looking way into the future, or an annual repetitious procedure that produces plans that are never referred to. Project planning is done very close to the implementation of that plan; it soon will be put to the test—it is 'active planning'. Project planning is akin to completing a well constructed cryptic crossword or putting together a particularly complex jigsaw puzzle. It is challenging, real and a 'living process' which can be enjoyed if approached with a positive mental attitude.

In comparison with other types of business planning, project planning is paradoxical. With sales planning it is not known what the outcome will be, it can only be planned for and then skills and experience applied to drive for it. With project planning the exact end is known from the beginning. But it has never been done before. So with sales planning what we will eventually get isn't known—but we know how to go about getting it; with project planning we do know what we will get but we are not sure how we will get it.

How long to produce a Defensible Plan?

Experience of project management indicates that thorough planning takes between 8 and 10 per cent of total project time. So a task that will take about a month to do (20 working days) should have two days set aside for planning. If enough time is not allocated for planning at the beginning of the project then a lot more time will be required later when trying to implement; not just in resources but in personal stress. So set up to succeed—from the beginning.

In the following chapters each of the steps in a Defensible Plan is addressed separately.

The structure of the book allows for working on a 'live' project, applying the techniques being taught as you go. If you do not have a live project then you can either follow the examples given or plan an imaginary project that may become 'live' in future.

Although, by definition, all projects are different, the structure of one successful project plan can act as a very effective template when planning another.

Defining your project

I keep six honest serving men
(They taught me all I knew)
Their names are What and Why and When
And How and Where and Who.

Poem *The Elephant's Child* by Rudyard Kipling (by kind permission
of A P Watt Ltd, Literary Agents on behalf of The National Trust
for Places of Historic Interest or Natural Beauty).

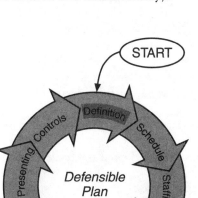

What are you being asked to do?

In operational work when you are asked to keep an existing process
going, it is in most cases repetitive. Constantly trying to improve the
process, make it faster, better quality, use less resources and so on. It is
seldom that you are given the opportunity of setting up a process from
the beginning. You are more often in the position of taking over what
already exists.

Project working is different; it deals with a finite quantity of work.
You are able (in most cases) to start at the beginning and set up the
project right from the start. Mostly you are not used to doing this. You
are challenged to think in ways that operational working does not

prepare you for. How do you start at the beginning—and what is the beginning? The beginning of a project is the project definition.

Defining your project is the first step of your Defensible Plan and it needs some careful thought. To deliver a project well you must understand *why* it is needed and *what* it is for *at the start* of the planning process; a seemingly obvious statement but project managers are often in the position of not fully understanding what it is they are being asked to do. There can be many reasons for this. Vague instructions from project initiators can turn into vague project objectives. Time may not have been taken to define clearly what is in the mind of the initiator. Or the original request may have passed through a number of hands and the real need has become distorted along the way. A good instruction could have been given but the recipient failed to record it correctly.

The unsure project manager may be hoping that understanding will come later as the plan gets built. For these reasons, and others, the project definition should be written down. The project manager needs to look at the big picture and *must* understand:

■ *why* the project is needed and where it fits in the organisation's objectives;
■ *what* needs to be done and what the project will achieve.

Inappropriate clarity

There is a temptation to move away quickly from this big picture thinking process to *how* something can be done—before the *why* and *what* are properly understood. This is because of the discomfort felt, stemming from lack of clarity—living in fog. This invariably leads to an over reliance on assumption. The wrong conclusions are then 'forced' on the project.

For example, I worked with a project team which was given the following written project brief:

Various departments are using a number of technological methods (fax, voice-mail, etc.) for external and internal communications. Investigate what is being used and make recommendations about how you should proceed.

The team were asked to come up with some recommendations and after four months reported:

All expenditure for communications equipment, including all computers, fax machines, mobile phones and associated software should be authorised and controlled by the IT department.

The report addressed the controlling of the purchase of communication equipment. In the opinion of the senior manager who had asked for recommendations, it was not what the project team had been asked to do. Indeed, the team had gone ahead and addressed what they *could* control rather than what they *should* have addressed—the shortcomings of the corporate communications strategy. The brief was not clear and was open to misinterpretation but the project team had not attempted to clarify it with the senior manager.

The *why* was not understood—what were the circumstances that brought about the need for this project? The team had assumed it was about cost control/reduction. In fact it was about effective communications inside and outside the organisation—which medium to use for which communication—fax, e-mail, voice-mail, etc.—to bring commonality to a diverse group of companies. Cost was a part of the project, not the project itself. If the wording of the brief had been clearer then confusion might not have arisen. It is, therefore, the job of the project manager to bring clarity to the project before work starts.

Depending upon your seniority and experience, you may have a natural reluctance to question or challenge other people and in particular your boss. But in achieving project definition you need to ensure that all are thinking alike. To make certain of this write down:

■ *why* the project is wanted and what are the circumstances that brought about its need;
■ *what* this will do to solve the problem;
■ *how* it is to be done—with objectives;
■ *who* is involved or impacted by the project.

Have this written definition signed off by the project initiator. (In the absence of such a briefing document there is nothing to stop you drafting it yourself.)

Guidelines for defining projects

Project definition is not a ten-minute job; creating a good definition even for a 'small' project is expressed in hours rather than minutes and substantial projects can take days of effort. So ask for enough time to be briefed correctly, don't be fobbed off with two minutes in the corridor. It is not an easy thing to do but the investment of time and thinking effort at the beginning is rewarded by an absence of rework and resulting poor morale later on. The goal is to ensure that all stakeholders understand the project and see the goals in the same way.

You may be defining a project yourself and no sponsor exists. In this case ask an objective colleague to look at your draft—does it make sense to them? To bring clarity to your project, start at the *why* ensuring that you understand where the project came from.

Why? What circumstances?

This is 'big picture' thinking. Ask questions as to why you are where you are and why this project is needed.

- Why does the organisation need this project?
- What is the business case?
- What is the background and history that got you to where you are now?
- What triggered this project at this time?
- What is the problem/opportunity being addressed?
- Where does it fit in the organisation's objectives?
- Are there any other related projects running?

Once it is understood where the project came from and the nature of the problem that needs solving, move on to *what* questions.

What? What are the options?

This *what* is about logical thinking as opposed to the big picture thinking of the previous paragraph. The iteration between the two styles of thinking will give the *context* of your project (Figure 2.1). Will this project resolve the issue identified?

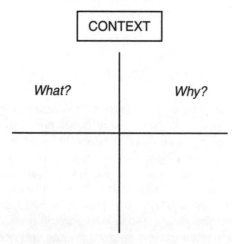

Figure 2.1   Project context

Ask the question:

- What does the organisation want to do about it?
- What is this project to do and what are the options?
- What is it not to do?
- What changes are expected as a result of this project?
- What return on investment is the organisation looking for and how will it be measured?
- What will the success of this project look like?
- What other options were considered?
- What factors were of prime importance in reaching this plan of action?
- What are the deliverables and expectations?

The full understanding of the *why* and the *what* will provide the *context* of the project.

Having chosen one of your options you can move on to *how* you could do the project. This is where you can start addressing the *task* itself.

How? How will it be done?

The thinking style narrows down to a more detailed and step by step approach when considering which various options eventually lead to a plan.

- How should it be approached?
- What objectives should be set?
- What measurable outcomes are foreseen?
- What will the tangible results be?
- When is it wanted by?
- What resources are there?
- What is the budget?
- What authority do you have?
- What are the boundaries and the priorities?

Detailed answers about *when* the project is done and *where* it will be done is also determined under this task heading. Continuing discussions helps find out *who* will be affected by the project. Not just those who are involved in carrying it out but also those who will be impacted by the project in any way. These people are referred to as stakeholders. The answers to *why* and *who* gives an idea of the *process* to be followed:

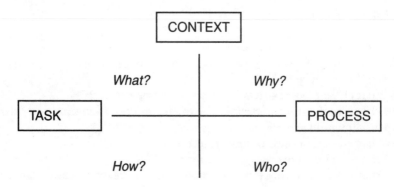

Figure 2.2   Task and process

- Is this the project for an individual in charge?
- Are there team elements?
- What skills should the people have?
- Should IT be used? Will staff work well together?
- Can you train them?
- Do you have dedicated time, or do these people have to do a full-time job as well as this project?
- How are you to manage them?
- What assumptions have been made and what are the constraints?

Task and process (Figure 2.2) can be added to the model of the project definition. There is often tension between the action-oriented task thinking and the more reflective process thinking which asks for the holding of actions until all the elements of the project definition have

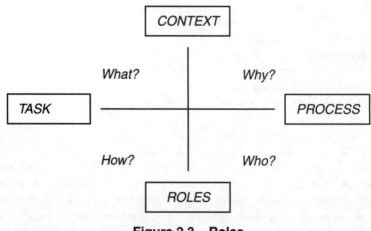

Figure 2.3   Roles

been thought through. You are then left with the question *who?* to be answered.

Who? Who is impacted by this project?

■ Who are the stakeholders and how do you keep them happy?
■ What would those involved like to see happen?
■ What are the political dimensions?
■ Who is in support?
■ Is there anyone who is against this project succeeding?
■ Where do you need to tread carefully?
■ Has this project been tried before and if so what was the outcome?
■ Are there any no-go areas?

Knowing about the *how* and the *who* will also give a picture of the *roles* (Figure 2.3) needed on the project team and *who* might fit them.

In Figure 2.3 note that roles is placed at the bottom. Each person involved in the project has two roles, one from *how* and one from *who*. The *how* is a functional or expertise role, the particular technical skills that person brings to the party. The *who* role is the membership of the project team and the contribution that each person makes to the

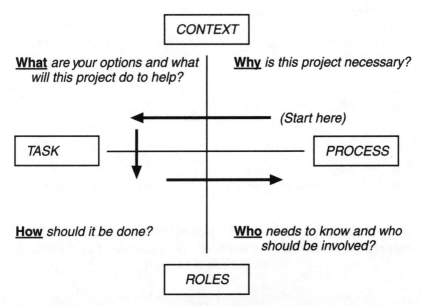

Figure 2.4   The sequence to produce a project definition

Background (Why?)

Independent subsidiaries and divisions are using several technological methods of communicating between themselves. There now exists (in addition to paper based communications) voice banks, electronic mail, the Internet, mobile telephones, pagers, faxes etc. All are used without reference to compatibility. We are now in the situation of decisions being delayed whilst vital communications are lost between these media. Although this problem is confined to internal communications at present, it is only a matter of time before our customers will be impacted—if indeed this is not already the case. This project will address this issue.

Scope (What?)

This project has been initiated to improve communications between the divisions to ensure that a lasting communications strategy is written, agreed and implemented by all divisions. The strategy should include recommendations that:

1. a minimum of efficient and effective communications tools and techniques are used throughout the organisation;
2. these tools and techniques are common to all divisions by the end of next year;
3. a process is set up to control future purchases of communication equipment to ensure compatibility and policy adherence by the end of next year.

Project objectives (How?)

This project is to:

■ gather data about what exists in the divisions;
■ analyse the data to assess areas of accidental compatibility;

Figure 2.5 An example of a project definition which addresses corporate communication within the UK operations of the ACME organisation (fictional)

- look for and report on best practice in the market;
- produce options for action and associated costs;
- submit its report including research, options and recommendations for the preferred option, together with an outline implementation plan to the Project Sponsor by 31st July;
- make a 20 minute presentation of recommendations to the Operations Board on the 8th August.

The People (Who?)

You have available the members of your project team and any other resource you can persuade to help. There is no budget for this work and you are expected to continue with your existing work during the term of the project.

Please do not extend your work beyond dedicated interdivisional communication equipment and processes in this project. However opinion on related hardware and software issues would be welcomed.

This project will have an impact on the IT department especially in the area of hardware purchase. You should talk with the head of IT and gain his agreement to your overall approach before you finalise your plan. It is recommended that you seek an adviser from this department as a member of your project team. You should also consider the needs of all those, both internal and external, who may be impacted by the results of this project and ensure that their problems and opinions are sought.

Please submit and discuss your project plan with me on 18th February.

Signed ....   Signed ....

Project Initiator   Project Manager

Date   Date

working of that team. Successful project managers consider both aspects. There is little point in bringing together the best operators in the business if they are unable to cooperate with each other.

Summary

All of Kipling's 'honest serving men' have been used to good effect in the understanding of what it is that you are being asked to do. In trying to produce a project definition (see Figure 2.4 on page 23) you will go back and forth and up and down between the questions. The thoughts of *why* are tested for their reasoning in the *what*. The logic from the *what* is tested for viability or 'doability' by answering the questions about *how* it can be done and *who* is going to do it. Even having satisfied all three questions, the organisation's culture or the internal politics may render the project unworkable in the *who*. However, by following through this sequence you will have a clearer understanding of what it is that you are being asked to do.

Project definition

In Figure 2.5 a simple format is used to define a project. It is based on a real-life document used to communicate between divisions of an organisation. Such a document can be produced by you after discussions with the project initiator. If you are initiating it yourself then the document should still be drafted to clarify and demonstrate your thinking. It is not an attempt to sew-up the project entirely. Questions remain to be answered but the document is a good foundation from which to further plan a project.

Scheduling the work

Remember that time is money.
Benjamin Franklin *Advice to Young Tradesmen* (1748)

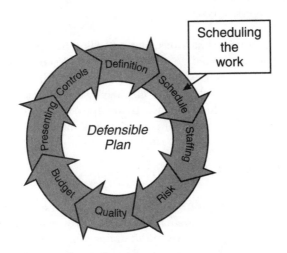

Having determined the full project definition and made sure that you have the necessary clarity of understanding between yourself and the organisation, work can be scheduled. This means your calculating how long both the project and the various parts of the project are going to take. And acknowledging Mr Franklin's perceptive advice from so long ago, it should be done in as little time as possible.

Building a picture of the project

It is necessary to build a picture of what the project 'looks' like. Just as an architect's drawing can picture the finished object, so the project plan should pictorially present the project.

There are lots of tools to help here but they do need some intelligent application or the application of the tool can become more important than managing the project. Don't fall into the common trap of becoming an expert in using project management software whilst failing to understand the project.

By following the process outlined here you will 'know' the project better and so you will enjoy greater confidence in the management of the project. Experience shows that the more that is done at this stage of planning, the easier the project will be to manage at the later planning and implementation phases.

In this chapter you will decide:

■ what work is involved;
■ how long it will take;
■ in what order it will be done.

This is where you begin the work that will allow for the negotiation of time and resources needed to do a good job. You are working on assumptions at this stage—it couldn't be anything else without some sort of plan. Even if a similar task has been done before, no two projects are exactly alike, different factors always come into play whether those factors are people, money, team members and so on.

Visualising your task

When you start assessing time and resources the project exists in your brain as one amorphous mass. It's hard to picture it and a sense of panic might arise every time you think about what has to be done. But if you break it down into some sort of logical structure then it can be easily understandable and manageable. To achieve this use Work Breakdown Structure (WBS).

WBS: What is it?

Imagine being on a trip to the supermarket. It is something that you don't do often, so you wander around the aisles with a shopping list (Figure 3.1).

─────────────── *John's Shopping List* ───────────────

sausages	apples	milk	juices
leg of lamb	light bulbs	bananas	cheeses
bacon	dusters	lettuce	yoghurt
spare ribs	w/up liquid	tomatoes	butter
hamburgers	soap powder	potatoes	margarine
cod	coffee	tea	cucumber
razor blades	single cream	coffee	brillo pads

Figure 3.1   Shopping list

You keep a lookout for items on your list in the hope that you can find them on the shelves. This becomes a rather long and frustrating task as you go back and forth looking for those items you missed first time around.

However, if you were to draw up a shopping list with the help of an experienced shopper, you would be advised to *break down* your list into categories as they are found in supermarket sections: meat, vegetables, cereals, dairy, detergents, etc., so each section is visited only once.

You now have a structure (Figure 3.2).

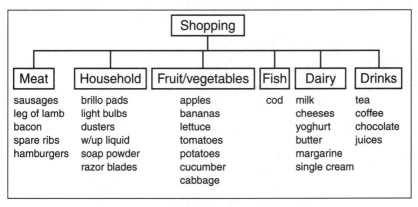

Figure 3.2   Shopping list breakdown

All that is needed now is the right order (Figure 3.3) for visiting the appropriate sections in the supermarket.

Additionally, your expert shopper may add value by advising on the best place to park, or which checkout is the fastest. You now have more chance of being both efficient and effective.

This is what WBS does: it takes a number of related tasks, puts them together and then applies some logic to get them in a sensible order for implementation. When you shop it may not be too important to plan the outing; the consequences for not doing so are not great, but it is not wise to apply the same *ad hoc* approach to your professional life.

Choices

The same choices exist for projects. You can either dash around hoping that you cover all bases, then crisis manage with all the pressure and angst for the whole project. Or you can stop and think it through at the beginning to produce a well-structured list, having had some help from people who know more than you.

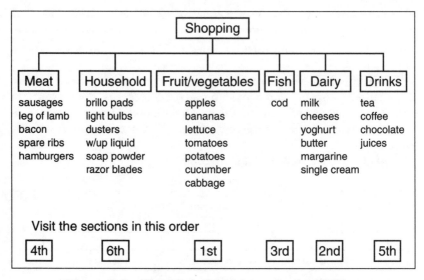

Figure 3.3   Establish the right order for visiting

Example

You have been tasked with the production of a marketing brochure for a new product, something you haven't done before. You have discussed with the project initiator your definition and have been asked to complete in one month. Your project is one of a number of coordinated tasks which are all to do with the launch of a new product. The programme has been broken down by function (Figure 3.4).

In Figure 3.4 marketing has been broken down further to show the projects that exist in that function. Each of them is a significant piece of work that will have to be broken down further for managing. The arrowed box is your project, a part of the marketing function which you must now break down into smaller tasks and more manageable chunks. You have not been given staff or formal line help. Sitting at your desk you are very much aware of your lack of knowledge but you give it a try anyway.

A brochure has copy and photographs. Marketing will have given you some sort of brief to work to; what design and how long it should be, who the brochure is for and how many copies will be printed.

Make a project plan (Figure 3.5).

It looks OK but is it?

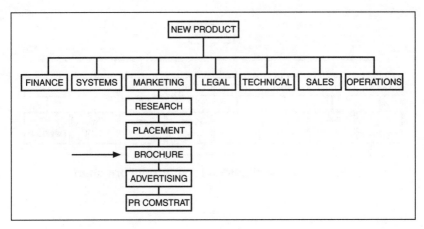

Figure 3.4   Project functions

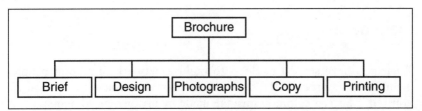

Figure 3.5   Project plan

Getting help

If you haven't done this before then you should get all the help you can and the best place to start recruiting this help is at the beginning. This is not the first brochure that your organisation has produced so there must be some expertise around. After a couple of phone calls the name Susan Ericsson is given as someone who has done a couple of brochures recently and rumour has it that she did a good job—she's friendly too. She accepts your invitation to lunch and in the canteen she gives you some help. Your initial breakdown isn't too bad and you haven't fallen into the trap of including too much detail. (You need to be looking at the main areas you are going to have to manage and shouldn't be worrying about the detail at this stage.) The key point Susan can help

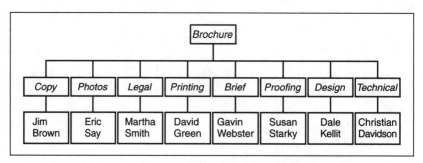

Figure 3.6   Add names to your network chart

you with is to be able to understand what has to be done so that you can personally manage it. You will have to rely on others but that doesn't mean that you abdicate responsibility or control.

Help network

What you have started to do is to build a network of helpful people. Your job is to produce the brochure but you don't have to do it all by yourself. This is a common mistake made by inexperienced managers. It leads to repeated mistakes and re-invention of the wheel. Getting help means getting other people involved in your projects.

Susan adds some boxes to your diagram and changes others. She also gives you the names of people she thinks can help and hints that she couldn't produce a brochure in four weeks! Add her names to your breakdown and create a relationship network chart (Figure 3.6).

Your network has eight activities that will need separate management. You can contact the names given to you by Susan and ask them for help. People seldom turn down a request for help, especially if it gives them the opportunity to demonstrate their abilities. Try and find one individual to help you with each activity that is new to you.

A good rule of thumb for the length of an activity is nothing longer than three weeks or about 100 hours of work. More than that and you may not have enough control if something goes wrong. You can accept much shorter lengths if the activity does not fall readily into another activity. For example, legal only takes a week but if you lumped it in with, say, proofing, then you are dealing with different people for different tasks and it therefore needs separate management.

Your help network can save you much grief all the way through your task and it is something that you should practise for all your management activities, not just project management. When you go along to see each of your contacts, take with you an activity description sheet (Figure 3.7). It will help you to gather the right information about what you need to know about the activity you are discussing as it requires each activity to be described.

The activity description sheet is largely self-explanatory but it is worth stressing a few points and these are discussed below.

Activity labels

These are used as a shorthand for the activities. They save you having to write out the name of the activity every time you wish to refer to it. They also tell, depending on the numbering system used, where the activity belongs in the project. A labelling system can be used in the same way as a numbering system in a report. In Figure 3.8 the 'D' is

---

1. *Name of Activity*
   Photography

2. *Activity Label*
   'D'

3. *Activity Deliverable*
   A set of approved Product Photographs

4. *Skills/Competencies*
   Professional photographer with product brochure experience

5. *Preceding Activities (Predecessors)*
   'A'

6. *Person Responsible*
   Eric Wright

7. *Typical Duration in Days (Hours)*
   10 Days for 2 staff

8. *Special Permission/Actions*
   Photographic proofs—Product Marketing Manager

9. *Notes*
   Collection and return of product from R&D by photographer

10. *Estimated Costs*
    £2200

11. *Activity Manager*........   *Task Manager*........

Figure 3.7   Activity description sheet

LABEL	DESCRIPTION	DURATION (DAYS)	STAFF REQ'D	PREDECES-SORS
A	BRIEF	5	1	-
B	DESIGN	10	1	A
C	TECHNICAL	5	2	A
D	PHOTOGRAPHY	10	2	A
E	COPY	15	2	B,C
F	LEGAL	5	1	E
G	PROOF	10	1	D,F
H	PRINT	5	1	G

Figure 3.8   Activity data summary

about photography so every label that starts with a D has to do with photography. D1 might be location choice, D2 could be hire special lighting equipment and so on.

There is nothing to stop you using straight numeric, 1-1, 2-1, etc., going down to a third level, 1-1-4 or 2-1-6 if your task is more complex.

Activity deliverable
When you complete this you must ensure that you do express it as an outcome, preferably something tangible.

Preceding activities
These (predecessors) are the deliverables that must be in hand before the activity in question can start. In this case you cannot start the photography until you have the brief in your hands.

Person responsible
You will need your persuasion skills to secure commitment to your plan, so the person advising you is the best person to be responsible. You tend to be more careful over plans you yourself are going to deliver. If you cannot achieve this then ask for another name.

Duration

How long can cause heated debate during task scheduling. Estimating how long an activity will take is not an exact science so you are unlikely to get exact answers but you need enough accuracy to be able to defend your plan. It is often a case of asking the right questions of your adviser. When you are having difficulty getting an answer, try 'bracketing'. Ask what the maximum time and minimum time for the activity might be, then choose a point midway between the two answers.

If you are counting in weeks, an extra day can be added to an existing week in the hope that it will be absorbed. If you are counting 5 days as a project week then 6 days can hardly be counted as 2 weeks. However, if there are 2 days or more to be added to a week, then a full extra week has to be added; it is not safe to assume that 2 days can be absorbed. So 7 days becomes 2 project weeks. At this stage, do not worry about the 3 days left over, they will be used later in the process of building the Defensible Plan.

These estimates are not cast in stone at this stage. You can go back later but be as accurate as you can.

In the completion of these tasks it is important that you understand enough about each activity so that it can be managed. It can be daunting to sit in front of a professional expert discussing a subject you know nothing about. For example, if there is a legal aspect to your task you don't need to know the law but you do need to know what has to be done in practice, what are the steps that have to be gone through, and how long each step will take.

Activity data summary

By the time you have created a sheet for each activity, you will be getting a good feel for the project and your confidence levels will be rising. It is a short step to producing a brief summary of all the activity sheets into one manageable document (Figure 3.8).

How does it all fit together?

Using Figure 3.8 you can show how all the parts of your project fit together. The Predecessors column shows how one activity links to all the others in the task. If your project is a simple one and you know exactly what you are doing, then you can produce this activity summary omitting the separate activity description details, which will provide you with a more workable project network diagram (Figure 3.9). Start with activity A and then work forward. (If you are doing it for the first time

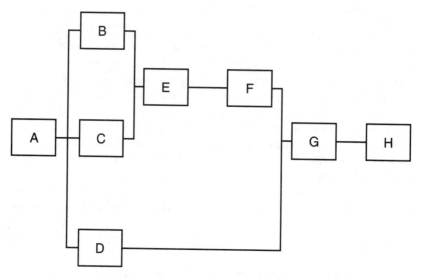

Figure 3.9   Project network diagram

then use pencil and eraser, it is unlikely that you will get it right first time.)

Already some useful information is emerging. Activities B, C and D can all start together provided A has been done. Therefore there is no point in worrying about E until B and C are well started, and so on.

How long is it going to take?

To work out how long it will take, add some more data to the network; add the duration for each activity from the activity summary sheet, to the bottom right-hand corner of each activity box (Figure 3.10).

Forward pass

Having done that carry out a *forward pass* calculation (Figure 3.11). It is quite simple but the process tells a lot. Starting at the outside top left of activity A place a 0 (zero), add the duration to the 0 and place it in the outer top right of the activity box. Carry that number forward to the next activity box and keep going until the end of the project.

Having carried all the numbers forward it can be seen that the project will take 50 days or 10 working weeks. Notice also that activities B and C have different finishing times so pass forward to E the *higher* number

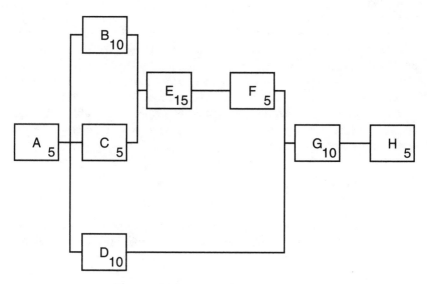

Figure 3.10   Add duration times

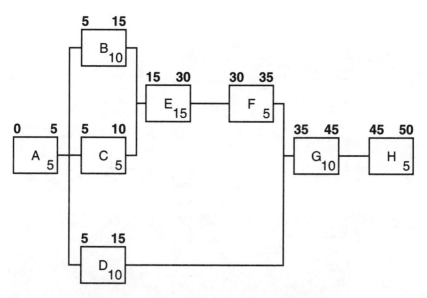

Figure 3.11   Forward pass calculation

(the earliest finish day). You can now tell the earliest that an activity can be started (top left) and the earliest it will be finished (top right). Activity F can't start until day 30 or the end of week 6 and it won't be finished until the end of week 7.

At this stage there are some broad questions that can be answered. First, as things stand this project will take about 10 weeks so it cannot be done in 4 weeks. Of course, reducing the project is possible but from 10 weeks to 4 weeks is too much. However, at this stage continue on with the process.

Backward pass

There is more that can be learned from the project network. Carry the 50 days' duration from activity H down to the bottom right-hand corner of the same square then do a *backward pass* back along the network (Figure 3.12).

You may be wondering why this exercise is necessary as the duration answer remains the same. That is true but look at activity D. The earliest that it can be started is day 5 or the end of week one. But the latest it can be started is day 25 or the end of week five. If for some reason it is not started until day 15, there is no need to panic because there are still 10 days to spare. The pressure eases further as a picture is built up of what should be happening at what time. You are no longer assuming that everything has to be done immediately.

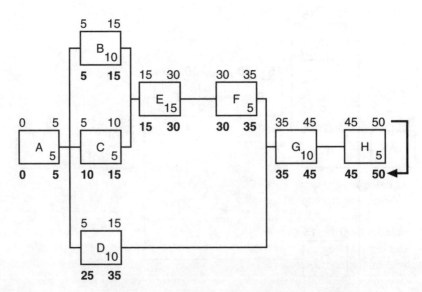

Figure 3.12   Backward pass (as bold arrow)

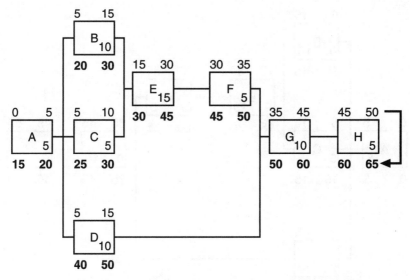

Figure 3.13   Fixing a future date (as bold arrow)

Working to a fixed future date

A backward pass can also be useful when you want to finish your project at some future point (Figure 3.13). All you need is a backward pass from the finish date you want to use. Let's say the desired finish is in three months' time (13 weeks or 65 days). Change the 50 for 65 then do a backward pass through the project network.

The latest start for activity A is now 15 days or the end of the third week from now. As long as the project is under way by then, you'll make it.

Room to manoeuvre

Going back to the 50 days forwards and backwards, *slack* or *float* can be calculated (Figure 3.14). This is the flexibility in the plan.

Subtract the top left number from the bottom left number for each activity thus working out the slack. Put this new number in the inside bottom left of each box.

This number tells how many working days the activity can be delayed without affecting the overall project plan. In Figure 3.14 there are only two activities that have slack, C and D. The rest have no slack and are therefore on the *critical path*.

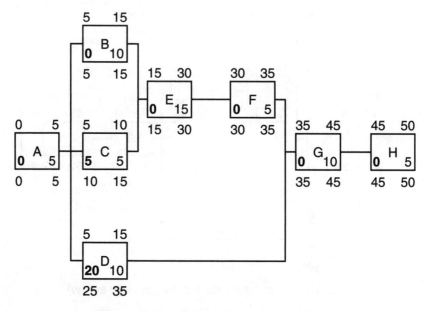

Figure 3.14   Calculating slack or float

Critical path

The critical path (Figure 3.15) is very important to the project manager, it is the longest route through the network and joins all activities without slack. Therefore it is essential that all the activities on the critical path are completed on time if the project is to deliver to schedule.

The dotted line in Figure 3.15 follows the critical path of this network. As you haven't done this before, it would make sense to also include all activities with one week or less slack and then add them to the critical path.

Reducing the length of the project

Of course it is all well and good if the project is within the time scale you have, however arbitrary. But what happens if you are over the given time scale? First, go back to the people who have been helping and ask them if there is any way that activities can be either shortened or done differently. For example, making a start on one activity before its predecessor is completely finished. Activity E might be able to start halfway through activity B and so on. Ask your helpers to tell you how it can be done. Remember that the only activities that will affect the

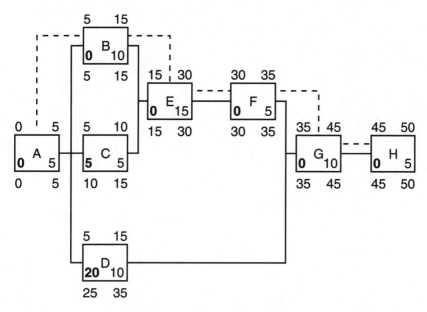

Figure 3.15   Critical path

length of the project are those activities on the critical path, the others will have no impact unless they affect the critical path itself.

Checking the plan so far

Having done all this careful work go back to your helpers and show them what you have done. Make sure that you concentrate on the critical path; it is here that any schedule is vulnerable. Issue your network diagram to all those involved in the project and tell the people who are on the critical path that their role is vital to the success of the project. Give them a last chance to change their estimate and listen hard to what they have to say. If they want more time, now is the time to give it to them.

By now you will have a picture of the relationships between the activities in your project. You are starting to find out the critical areas of your task and you already have an idea of where you should be at any given time in the project schedule. Knowing where you should be at a given point of time is a great aid to stress reduction. Later in the book you will be shown how to find out *where you are* in the project, as opposed to *where you think you are*. You now know how to estimate the resources needed to successfully deliver the project under control.

Estimating resources needed

CHAPTER

4

Castles in the air—they are so easy to take refuge in. So easy to build too.
Henrik Ibsen *The Master Builder*

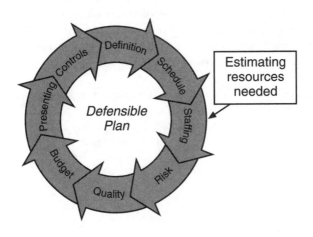

How many people?

You are now becoming very knowledgeable and familiar with the project which will stand you in good stead as planning is continued.

When looking at the people needed to staff the project it is important to start at the beginning. This may seem obvious, but it is all too easy to consider what is possible in the way of securing resources rather than what is needed. And it is all too easy to restrict resource planning using knowledge of what is available. It is better to clear minds of constraints so that a true assessment can be made of what is needed to deliver the project. Castles in the air are built when project managers underestimate the resources they need for the work to be done. Always keep in mind:

By first working out what is needed in full, any constraints can be accommodated later by adjusting the plan. In this way you will know exactly the impact any reduction in needed resources will have on the project.

If you tell yourself that you will not get this or that resource, you will never have a clear view of what is actually needed. Additionally, you may be surprised by being able to secure more resources than you thought possible. It is much easier to assert needs when confident of the accuracy of plans. The Defensible Plan builds confidence in project managers—and confident project managers tend to secure the resources they need.

To assess the people resources needed, transfer the information from the logic network to a bar chart. This will let you count the numbers and ensure that you make best use of the minimum resources typically available to project managers. To do this add the number of people needed for each activity to the top left corner of each box on the network diagram; this information is on your activity summary sheet (see Figure 4.1).

Notice that you are still working from this single network document which continues to tell more and more about the project. You can use this information to produce a schedule using a bar chart or Gantt chart as they are sometimes called. Gantt is the name of the man who first used bar charts in projects.

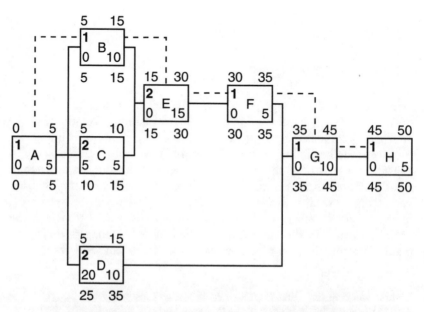

Figure 4.1   Add the number of people needed

Bar or Gantt Charts

To create a bar chart look at activity A on the logic network in Figure 4.2. It will take 5 days (a working week) and will need one person to do it. On the bar chart draw a box, the length of which indicates the duration of this activity. Inside the box put the label of the activity and the number of staff needed. In the case of the first activity, add 'A1'. For task C add the one week of slack by extending the length of the box using dotted lines, then insert C2 to indicate the activity and the number of people involved. Continue to work your way along following the task numbers and the logic network until it is complete (Figure 4.2). By adding down the numbers of people required for the activities in any week (ignoring slack weeks), the total number of people needed for the project can be seen—as you make progress along the planned route. At the moment the maximum resources needed in the staff plan is 5 people for week 2.

Levelling the staff plan

Using Figure 4.2, it can be seen that, by taking the total of the resources needed for each week, 19 person weeks of effort are needed. For the second week 5 people will be needed but only for one week. This can be displayed by creating a resource profile (Figure 4.3).

The profile has a marked peak in week 2. Peaks are expensive both in staff hours and in project managers' time. Therefore, the profile needs to be levelled to reduce the resources required by spreading activity throughout the project. Levelling makes the project easier to manage, for example, rather than four people coming all at the same time for briefing on the project and on their own particular activities, they can join in ones and twos. It is unlikely for such a short task that five staff would be available for just one week—it is just not defensible. Life should be made easier for those departments who are giving people to the project.

Project levelling is done by taking up slack or by moving the activities around within the logic network. In the brochure example there is slack in activities C and D. You can talk with the Technical and Photography activity leaders, to find out if they can do the work with one person in exchange for more time to do the work. In this case you are fortunate and the answer is yes to both, so take up some slack and reduce the manning peak (Figure 4.4).

Although the person weeks of work has remained the same, the maximum resource is now 3 instead of 5.

Slack has been taken up in activity C by reducing the staff from 2 to 1.

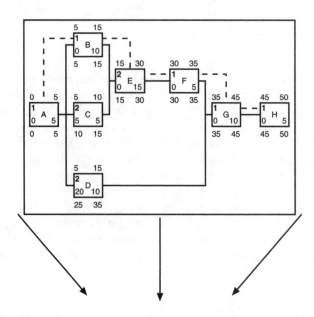

Week	No									
1	2	3	4	5	6	7	8	9	10
A 1										
	B 1	1								
	C 2									
	D 2	2								
			E 2	2	2					
						F 1				
							G 1	1		
									H 1	
1	5	3	2	2	2	1	1	1	1

Total people required by week ⟶

Figure 4.2   From network to bar chart

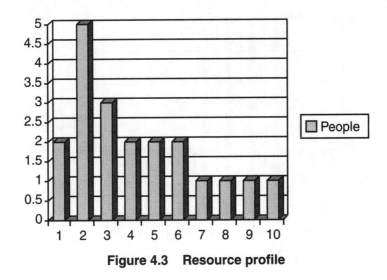

Figure 4.3   Resource profile

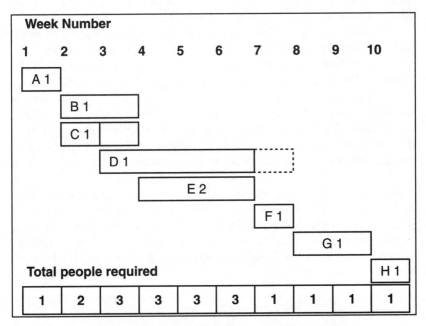

Figure 4.4   Reducing the manning peak

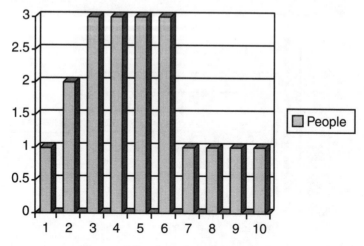

Figure 4.5   Level resources plan

In activity D the start has been delayed by one week and two weeks of slack taken up by reducing the number of people from 2 to 1. Now draw the new profile of the project (Figure 4.5).

The project profile is 'smooth', it has no jagged peaks. You can go back to the activity leaders of B and C and tell them to do the activities with one person and to take twice as long for each as was originally planned. This process frees up resources for other work and reduces stress on the project leader. The first resource plan saw four new people join the project in the second week. Lots of briefing would have been needed as well as considerable amounts of time for people to bed in to their projects. The second smoother profile sees one person joining at any one time which means that the project manager can induct them more easily.

Resource levelling has its costs. It has been done at the expense of slack. As a general guide look for a remainder of some 10–20 per cent slack after smoothing the project. You can now see how important it is to resist the temptation to take up slack too early in the planning process. If there had been no slack there would have been little room for manoeuvre at this stage.

Using technical support to reduce resources needed

Many activities can be impacted by the use of technology; this in turn will impact favourably on the resources need. For example, if a concrete floor is to be laid in a house two people would be needed, one to mix the concrete and one to lay it. However, if technology is introduced—a cement mixer—staff can be reduced to one while getting the job done in more or less the same time. But the person employed must be able to use the mixer or nothing will have been gained.

For example, I am writing this book using Microsoft Office on a laptop computer. This means that I am typing directly into the machine and that I am producing the graphics by myself using MS Office. I can therefore reduce the duration of many of the activities in the project plan for my book *provided I can use the technology*. I don't need a typist to convert my manuscript or a graphics designer to do the illustrations but if I cannot make best use of the software then there will be little change in my plan. If you plan to use higher technology to reduce resources or shorten duration, then ensure that you plan for the skills being available in the Human Resources plan later on.

A word of caution about slack

You have been using total slack throughout this exercise. The more eagle-eyed reader may have spotted a flaw in using total slack. In Figure 4.6 notice that activity D takes 4 weeks. Activities B and C together take 3 weeks. Therefore, A to E has a critical path of 4 weeks—the longest route is the critical path. But in taking the duration of B and C then adding the slack allocated to each, the answer is 5 weeks.

The problem comes from the allocation of the total slack to both B and C. If the task leaders of B and C both took up the slack given to them, E would be one week late in starting. It is the project manager's job to ensure that this double counting is removed. A simple way to do it on the network is to subtract the earliest finish of a project (outside top right), from the earliest start of the next project (outside top left), placing the answer in the inside top right of the box. In Figure 4.7 C is the only task with *free* slack. As project manager you can decide if this is what you want.

Look carefully at the network, especially at the critical path and ensure that you allocate free slack in the way that you want to control the project. Free slack is a considerate way of managing a project schedule. It asks task leaders not to take up slack at the expense of the next task leader. For example, B has a week of total slack but no free slack.

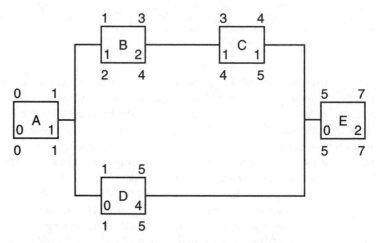

Figure 4.6   Using total slack

If B wants to use that week the leader of C must be informed and indeed may need to negotiate the sharing of the slack.

A word of caution about software

The more experienced reader will know that there are perfectly good software programs such as Microsoft Project or Project Management Workbench that will build networks and bar graphs for you. By all

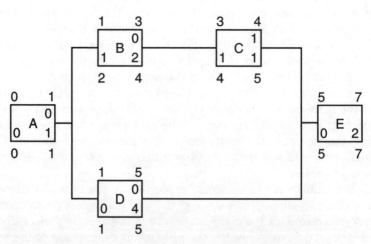

Figure 4.7   Simple subtraction exercise

means use them *once you have understood the concepts*. Too many inexperienced project managers buy software in the expectation that it will do much of the work for them. A word processor will not write a book; software will not deliver a project. They operate logically only when the person using them is using his/her own instinct and personal experience. Have a care that you do not spend more time getting to grips with software than you do in planning the project.

This book is about understanding the common sense concepts of project management, not about the use of IT. If you can fully understand the concepts then you will be able to use them wisely. Too many project managers both experienced and inexperienced, spend too much time entering data into software programs and not enough time leading their projects. Most answers lie with people not computers.

However, the information given by good software packages can be most useful in saving time for the project manager who has *first* understood the project schedule.

Summary

The bar chart or Gantt chart further builds on the picture of the project. You can 'see' how many people you need and when they are needed for best efficiency and effectiveness. Together with the network diagram, you have the means to present a picture of the project given and the time that is needed to do it well. The bar chart allows you to know what should be happening in any given week and, as project manager if you see a particularly heavy week, the work in other areas can be adjusted to accommodate the heavy load. Graphics provide a clear way of representing a project and are therefore good communication tools.

Planning for project leadership

CHAPTER

5

'I wonder men dare trust themselves with men.'
William Shakespeare *Titus Andronicus*

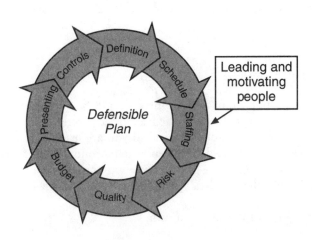

Up to now we have concentrated very much on the logical aspects of project planning, the schedule, the critical path, resource levelling and so on. This is all well and good but ultimately the plan will be delivered by people who at the moment are no more than ciphers on a page. Now is the time to consider them as people with needs and wants which are to be met if you wish to get the best out of them.

In this chapter we look at planning for leadership in two parts: first, a model for addressing leadership in project management and, second, the application of the model in projects.

The model

During the levelling process you have been allocating individuals to work together on activities on the huge assumption that all will be well between them and that they will maximise output to meet the needs of the project. Most of them have had the experience of working in happy teams which work well and get the job done. On the other hand most will also have had the unhappy experience of working in dysfunctional teams which struggle to get anything done, usually in a rather unpleasant atmosphere.

You are moving away from the purely logical and analytical thinking of step-by-step planning of events towards the less tangible needs of people and teams.

The thinking of John Adair (*The Skills of Leadership*, Gower, 1984) helps with the leadership of projects. To get the best out of people consider how to get the project done with and through them. In other words how to lead.

According to Adair, leaders should address three key areas:

1. Task.
2. Team maintenance.
3. Individual needs.

Each is equally important and all three should be kept in balance with each other. They can be visualised as three overlapping circles and described as 'the three circles of need'. If you are leading a project, each of the three circles should be given equal prominence. If one of the circles starts to dominate—grows bigger at the expense of the other two—it is likely that leadership problems will arise from the smaller circles.

Let's take each of the circles in turn.

Figure 5.1   The three circles of need

Task

The logical and analytical needs of the project have largely been addressed before reaching this point: what has to be done, outputs for

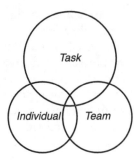

Figure 5.2   Distortion of circles caused by overemphasis on one activity

each activity, for how long, with how much and in what order are all planned. But once you start on implementation ensure that you focus on the meeting of deadlines on the critical path, etc. But not to the exclusion of all else.

For example, if the project leader decides that all effort is to be aimed at ensuring that tasks are delivered, regardless of the impact on people, then the task circle will grow large (Figure 5.2) at the expense of either one or both of the other circles.

In such circumstances the leader will encounter individual motivation problems and a lack of team cohesion. The task-oriented manager may think that that is an acceptable price to pay for the delivery of the project. But, ultimately, there will be unacceptable consequences. The political demise of Margaret Thatcher provides a good example. Ignoring political preferences, most people would agree that she was a highly effective but not necessarily popular Prime Minister. She got things done. But, by the end of her final term in office, not one minister had survived her Cabinet. On more than one occasion she chose to publicly undermine her own minister, who happened not to agree with her on a particular matter. Ultimately the situation arose where she lost her Chancellor and her Economic Adviser on the same day. The Cabinet was split on a number of issues and any notion of it being a collective decision-making body was lost under Mrs Thatcher's absolute confidence and dominance.

Whether she was right or not is secondary to the fact that many in her own government saw her as inflexible and dogmatic. The task circle had grown large at the expense of the needs of powerful individuals and the maintenance of the team as a whole. Even as she prepared to leave Downing Street for the last time she was reported as saying 'I gave them three elections what more did they want?' Mrs Thatcher's intense concentration on the task saw her brought down by her own colleagues through a combination of individual and team actions; two areas for which she seemed to have little time. In the organisations of today, whether business or political, delivering the task is not enough in the long term. *How* the task is delivered also determines success.

It is the leadership role of project managers to bring the three circles of need correctly into balance. So, when considering the resources for the project, look for more than technical proficiency and experience of people. Understand them as *individuals* and as a *working group* in the hope that you can build a team committed to delivering success in the task.

Individual needs

Committed individuals help deliver projects. Committed individuals are well motivated and to be motivated, they want their personal needs met. All of them need at least these criteria met:

- a clear and well understood objective;
- an expectation of achievement of that objective;
- confidence that they are capable of success through their own efforts;
- feedback about progress against their objectives;
- rewards for their successful efforts.

Motivated individuals must be well informed, involved, feel important to the success of the project and given opportunities to use their skills. If their skills can be further developed during the delivery of the project and they are aware of the increasing skill levels then they will be better committed to the leader and the project. They need to have the right incentives and rewards (which is not always about money). They need to be listened to so that they are contributing and feel that their ideas are being given a fair hearing. They want feedback and also to know that the boss is taking an active interest. They also want to be led in the right manner to suit their experience and stage of personal development.

To get commitment from individuals means meeting them one-to-one, face-to-face whenever possible. You will not deal effectively with individuals unless you meet them as individuals. Meeting them at a team meeting does not cover the needs of the individual. They need the opportunity to meet you at a specific time so that they can be given the opportunity to express their personal hopes and concerns for the project. They want to be aware of your interest in them and of your concern for their progress.

Motivating people takes time—if time is not allowed in the Defensible Plan for you to meet people as individuals then they can become de-motivated and you will not get their best efforts.

However, if you overdo individual attention then there is a risk that the task and the team will suffer as a consequence. A team can fail to form or become split due to unjustified perceptions of favouritism from those who demand less personal attention; and the project can suffer as a result of trying to over-satisfy all the needs of all the individuals.

In a sporting context you have seen the dropping of international stars for the coherence of the team as a whole. Reading the situation is the key to striking the right balance and you cannot do that unless you are meeting and talking with people in your team. This communication process applies whether you are working with or without authority over the people in the project team.

Team maintenance

Most tasks carried out at work involve working with other people. Each group member brings not only a set of particular skills to the group but also a set of values and behaviours. It is the application of these values and behaviours that determines whether an individual feels that he or she is a member of a team or just a contributor to a work group. But why have teams?

The resourcing of projects illustrates that, as the number of people is increased so the performance of the team should improve (Figure 5.3). Therefore, in simple logic the performance of the team is predictable as is shown by the straight line—the *expected result*. But you know that team life is not like that and one of two things will happen. First, if the

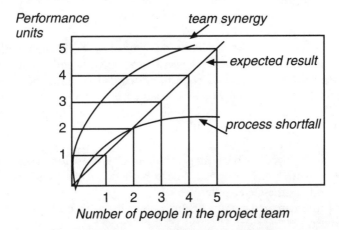

Figure 5.3   Project team working

team is able to combine the values and behaviours of the individuals in agreed actions, then *synergy* is achieved and the team performs beyond expectations. Secondly, and more often, the team does not know how to work together and synergy does not occur. The team performs below the expected level and that can be labelled *process shortfall* because the team does not have a process for working together. If a project manager has not been trained how to build teams then synergy happens by luck, or instinct, rather than by known and understood process.

To grow synergy by other than luck takes effort and care. A team cannot form unless it meets, works and communicates as a team with reasonable frequency. Bringing numbers of people together is costly in man hours and needs planning and budgeting. If it is not planned and budgeted then you will not have enough time for it within the project: the extra time needed will have to come from somewhere else—the evenings and weekends. If you pass on this pressure to the team then not only will you have not allowed time for synergy to occur to design, you may have created the conditions for resentment in the process. Hence, projects which demand that the team work nights, weekends and holidays can fail to produce anything other than acrimony between the team members.

The other side of the coin is where the maintenance of the team becomes all important; the cohesion of the team takes precedence over the task and the needs of individuals.

I have worked in such an organisation; the focus was very much on the people at the expense of the task. It was a great place to work with lots of support and interesting work but the very happy clients were not paying nearly enough for the organisation's excellent products. Everyone assumed that the money must be OK and that someone somewhere was looking after it. It took a new chief executive and a painful change of culture to put things right—just in time. The pendulum swung hard to the task area where it was needed to bring balance back to the three circles.

Leaders do need to consider the delivery of tasks through both individuals and teams. The actions needed to motivate individuals and to build teams take time, resources and effort. They cannot be pushed to one side. If they are, unwanted consequences for the project and the project leader can arise; for example, teams will not be built, the benefits of synergy will not be achieved, individuals will not be motivated and kept motivated. These meetings will not happen by chance, they are costly and so need to be well planned and allowed for in the budget. First, you work out how much time is needed and then you can budget and defend it—the Defensible Plan.

The project manager must spend some time with each participant in the project.

The application

In this second part of planning for leadership, we now look at some practical steps which can help prepare the ground for project implementation through motivated teams and individuals. This will give you a realistic, common sense understanding of how much time and resource you need to defend in the plans. *It is the omission of the techniques explained here that results in unworkable implementation plans.*

To do this we can return to the brochure example we used in Chapter 3. But whilst you have been thinking about leadership there has been a development in the marketing department. You have drawn attention to the fact that there is no methodology within the department for brochure production despite the fact that brochures are produced all the time. At present each brochure becomes an *ad hoc* project for some manager or another and the department continually has to climb the same learning curve. The skills of brochure production are not captured within the department and the same mistakes are being repeated time and again. No one seems to know how much these failings cost and there is growing dissatisfaction from internal customers. If this situation is not sorted out the reputation of marketing as a whole will suffer. The boss has listened to you and has recognised that the production of new product brochures has become a feature of the department and agrees that it should have a more professional footing.

As you are well into the planning of the latest brochure and you have been doing such a good job, you have been asked to form a standing project team (Figure 5.4) for brochure production. You have been given

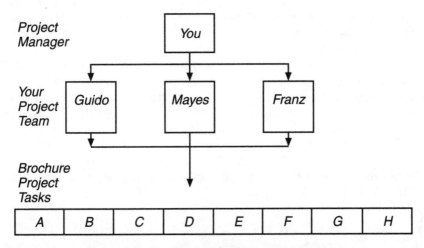

Figure 5.4   The standing project team

TEAM	Week Number	1	2	3	4	5	6	7	8	9	10
Name: **Guido**	Do task letter										
	Training and meetings										
Name: **Mayes**	Do task letter										
	Training and meetings										
Name: **Franz**	Do task letter										
	Training and meetings										

Figure 5.5   Implementation plan—outline format

three people to work part-time with you and it is hoped that, in due course, they too will become brochure project managers so growing and retaining the necessary skills in depth in the department. They are Jill Guido, Fred Mayes and Jim Franz; they have been involved in various parts of brochure production before but they will need training if they are to become project managers themselves. You are ambitious and self confident and you are finding project work stimulating so of course you accept. You have been asked to present the plan for achieving this additional goal in one week's time.

You are to deliver your brochure project using Jill Guido, Fred Mayes and Jim Franz to manage the tasks for you. So although you remain as project manager you have a team of three who will implement and control the project on a day-to-day basis.

To do this you will need an *implementation plan* (Figure 5.5) designed to show the allocation of resources to tasks in addition to other things impacting the project. The concept is simple; the plan will prompt you to issue instructions to the team on a week-by-week basis: who is to do what, where, when and with whom.

As illustrated, allocate week numbers along the top and names of people down the side. Using this document, complete these boxes (and others that you will see later) until you have a complete implementation plan. Do this in several steps.

Step one—allocate people to tasks

Focus on the *task circle* of the leadership model. To allocate people to tasks you need to know, amongst other things, two key pieces of information about each person:

1. Are they capable or *competent* to do the task—do they have the right skills?
2. What do they like doing and how do they like to work?

Let's deal with each in turn.

Competencies and skills

In assessing capability, draw up a *competency map* of the skills needed to work on the project. In this context, competence is the minimum skills needed to do a task well—the fundamentals needed to do the task. These competencies are simple and to the point. Do not confuse them with full organisational competency definitions—organisational competencies are far more complex and difficult to define than those discussed here. Competencies are used to help manage as well as lead by ensuring that there is clear understanding about what is needed to deliver the project.

For example, earlier it was seen that to produce a product brochure in today's litigious society, it needs to be legal, honest and true; and that another's copyright is not infringed by accident. You need the help of a lawyer. It could be said that all that is needed is someone trained in law so any lawyer will do. But in terms of project leadership this would be a mistake, albeit a common one. To succeed in delivering the brochure a rather better qualification than 'capable in law' is needed. A lawyer who is competent in copyright law and in the presentation of copy in brochures should be identified. Therefore in the project team you need someone who is *competent* in selecting experienced lawyers and then capable of managing the relevant legal processes required for brochures. Such a person does not need to know the law, but does need to know what the lawyer has to do in this field. Handing the process over to a lawyer and then sitting back is not enough.

The same applies to the photography tasks. The competency required is not just that of a professional photographer but of a professional photographer who is competent in producing high-quality brochure photographs. Again, in the project team you need competence in selecting and managing the photographic process for brochures so that the photographs arrive at the right time and are of the right quality. The project team member responsible does not need to know anything

Brochure Design	BD
Copy Writing	CW
Photography and Graphics	PG
Technical Writing	TW
Legal Liaison	LL
Final Proofing	FP
Printer Liaison	PL

Figure 5.6   Key competencies

about the technical aspects of photography but does need to know what it is that the photographer has to do.

Carrying on with this thinking and having looked at a typical brochure project, you have identified key competencies (Figure 5.6) necessary for those working on brochure production.

All the broad skills of a person competent in the production of a brochure should be covered here but it is important not to go into too much detail. Having identified the skills needed, measure the people against these competencies. If you know the people who are coming to the project then assess their competence against the identified areas. Remember that this is a subjective and perceptive process but by apply-ing the measure for all then you will use the same perceptive frame-work. If they are not known, gather information in a different way. Use the following sequence.

First, explain the competencies to each person and ask them to assess themselves against the competencies. Score out of 10 for each person, using the following values of competence:

1–2 low   3–4 below average
5–6 satisfactory   7–8 good   9–10 high.

If possible, ask a previous boss to assess each person. Make your own initial assessment and discuss the outcome with the person you are assessing. Review monthly following observation on the project.

When discussions are held with previous bosses seek specific informa-tion about a specific competency. In this way you will quickly build up a picture of the person with whom you will be working. Discuss find-ings with the person concerned at all times to show openness and re-assurance that this process is not a threat. Remain flexible and be

Name	BD	CW	PG	TW	LL	FP	PL
Guido	7	7	9	6	5	6	9
Mayes	3	4	8	5	8	6	6
Franz	2	3	7	0	8	0	4

Figure 5.7   Team competencies table

prepared to negotiate because after all you will be able to review the scores against performance when the project starts. It is important that the team members support this tool and see it as a help to their personal development.

Average the scores and you will have a good picture of the person. Having done this for individuals draw up a team table with everyone's competencies added (Figure 5.7). This table will tell you where the overall competence is low and therefore where close management will be necessary. It also shows you where training needs to be focused in the short term.

Building a table like this is more practical than at first may appear. Perceptions are remarkably similar. It is unusual for scores to be more than one mark apart in any given competency. Team members frequently give themselves lower competency scores than do their managers.

An example of a competency table in use is that of a first-line manager (supervisor) in the USA who went through this exercise for his team of 12 engineers. He worked out a set of competencies for the fundamentals of the job of a maintenance engineer fulfilling service contracts. He gave a copy of the competencies with the names of his people to his boss. After completion, they compared notes and found that in no instance were they more than one point away from each other.

In terms of sophisticated competency measurement this process is somewhat naive but it works. You are forced to think about the people and what they are able to do well and where they might need development. Having done this, add their competency information to your implementation plan (Figure 5.8).

You can now allocate people to tasks. Referring back to the activity summary sheet you can see that task A is the brochure brief and therefore you should assume that all the competencies will be needed. The person with the highest competencies is Jill Guido so it would make sense if she were to produce the brief. This is good task thinking but in terms of the leadership model you should consider the other two

TEAM	Week Number	1	2	3	4	5	6	7	8	9	10
Name: **Guido**	Do task letter										
BD CW PG TW LL FP PL 7 7 9 6 5 6 9	Training and meetings										
Name: **Mayes**	Do task letter										
BD CW PG TW LL FP PL 3 4 8 5 8 6 6	Training and meetings										
Name: **Franz**	Do task letter										
BD CW PG TW LL FP PL 2 3 7 0 8 0 4	Training and meetings										

Figure 5.8   Implementation plan—competencies added

circles—the individual and the team. You need to know more about Jill and the others.

Attitudes and preferences

You now move to addressing individual and team issues. From talking to the people, colleagues, friends, and the HR department, you can piece together some more information.

- ■ Guido.   Jill Guido is an excellent performer. She is very good at working with less experienced people. They learn a lot from her, and she has a good attitude towards the company which rubs off on the people working with her. She has about ten years' experience. Jill does not like working overtime when she is not convinced of the necessity. Her managers have often 'gone reactive' and asked her to work overtime when it did not make sense to her. She has tended to take time off after working overtime, but if she is counselled, and the reasons for overtime are explained, then she works well.

- ■ Mayes.   Fred Mayes is a solid worker who works long hours at reasonable productivity. He is rarely absent from work. Fred can be a bit difficult to get along with. He has a sharp tongue. He never accepts his performance appraisal. He argues that he should be rated higher in every category. In particular Fred does not get along with people with higher skills. This is probably because he thinks he is better than he actually is. Some people are not troubled by this and work well with him.

■ Franz.   Jim Franz has been with the company for one year. He
           appears to learn very fast and has done a good job on all
           work given to him. He gets along very well with co-
           workers. He has not been on board long enough for you to
           know much more.

You now have a better picture of the people and which combinations
are more likely to work. You will not always have the luxury of a
choice of people but, even if you have little choice, there are actions you
can take to help the chances of success. Going back to the project, in
summary:

■ Jill Guido has the most competence to do task A and, as she appears
  to be the best all-rounder, she should be pivotal in the delivery of the
  whole project. Therefore she should be in at the start of the project—
  allocate her to task A.
■ Fred Mayes, in the interests of team building for the future, could
  contribute well to task A working with Guido—provides he behaves
  himself.
■ Jim Franz is 'green' and needs to raise his skills but he is keen to do well.

The optimum choice for task A appears to be Jill working with Fred
Mayes. But this decision needs supporting—Jill will lead the task as she
has the greater experience and skills. Fred will not like this and will
become difficult unless actions to remedy the situation are taken.
  You can leave Fred and Jill to sort things out for themselves and hope
for the best; or you might like to prepare the ground to give a better
chance of success. In preparing the ground, there are a number of things
that can be done. Two of them are:

■ Meet with Jill and ensure that she is aware of your expectations of
  her. You can brief her about Fred and Jim.
■ Meet with Fred and brief him on the expectations about how you
  will run the project. Listen to him and then counsel him about how
  you expect him to work on the project—and how he is to work with
  the other team members—especially with Jill on the first task.

By taking these two actions you will help Jill and Fred to settle in to the
project and come to a workable relationship with each other.
  So, task-by-task, plot people by both their competencies and their
preferences on to the implementation plan (Figure 5.9). At the same
time make a note on the plan to remind yourself to hold individual
meetings with all at the start of the project.
  The eagle-eyed reader will have spotted that the smoothed resources
plan showed only one person for task A and that it should be complete

TEAM	Week Number	1	2	3	4	5	6	7	8	9	10
Name: **Guido**	Do task letter	A	B	B	E	E	E	F			H
BD CW PG TW LL FP PL 7 7 9 6 5 6 9	Training and meetings										
Name: **Mayes**	Do task letter	A	C	C	E	E	E		G	G	
BD CW PG TW LL FP PL 3 4 8 5 8 6 6	Training and meetings										
Name: **Franz**	Do task letter	A		D	D	D	D		G		
BD CW PG TW LL FP PL 2 3 7 0 8 0 4	Training and meetings										

Figure 5.9   Implementation plan—tasks added

by the end of week 1. In this case it was decided in the interests of team building to have all the staff involved under Jill's control. Although they may complete the task quicker, the main reason for the decision lies in the team maintenance circle. If the team can be built early then there will be benefit all the way through the project. When it comes to investing in people it is worth doing so as soon as possible in the project. Waiting until the middle of the project is too late. Jim Franz has also been added for a week to task G. Jim has a score of 0 for final proof and he is working with Fred so that he can observe what the competency is all about.

As Jim Franz is new and needs his skills improved before he can contribute fully to this and future projects, he needs to be trained. And so you can move to the second step which is the training plan.

Step two—training plan

To deliver the project you need competent people who can carry out the tasks. If they can't, they have to be given the competence through training. If they are not given the skills they need, individual morale will suffer—we all like to do a good job. The team will not build if individuals do not feel capable of contributing fully to the team's efforts.

To gain the most benefit from training investment carry out the training as soon as you possibly can. At the beginning of a project, people are still settling in and activity is likely to be lightest. Projects follow a predictable implementation cycle (Figure 5.10) which the project manager needs to consider at the planning stage.

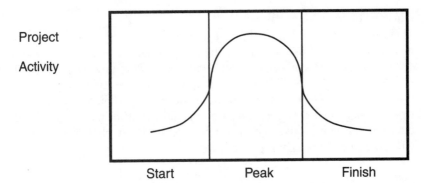

Figure 5.10 The implementation cycle

As time passes the activity on the project increases until it reaches a peak in the middle and then declines towards the end. It will likely match the levelled resources plan. The implementation cycle shows clearly that avoiding additional activity in the middle of a project is probably a good idea. But project managers often do just the opposite. They wait until problems develop, and just when most effort is needed on tasks, a problem reaches crisis point and has to be dealt with at the most inconvenient time.

For example, despite the importance of team work in projects, it is not unusual to observe project managers ignoring any consideration of team building actions until inter-personal relations in the team have become so bad that by the middle of the project the lack of co-operation is endangering the project delivery. Why not build the team at the beginning and benefit from the investment of early action all the way through? In the middle of the project when most activities are running, it is too late to build teams.

The implementation cycle shows the advantage of doing things early. There is little going on at project start up (in comparison with the peak) and having people away will have the least impact on the project. This is when to carry out any activities such as team building or training when maximum benefit for minimum disruption can be achieved.

Consider the training needed for all the people involved in the project—not just the inexperienced. Organisations grow when people get better at what they do. All managers and leaders have a duty to train their people. When busy with the pressures of other daily work it is all too easy to pass on the responsibility of training to others—which usually means it doesn't get done. Effective project managers give back their teams at the end of a project more capable than they were at the beginning. Someone took the responsibility for training your people for you, now it is time for you to reciprocate.

Choices of training activity

There are many training methods, some more effective than others. The most effective methods tend to be the most expensive but right now you are not concerned with cost—that comes later. Planning for everything means you will have a full picture of all the resources needed to deliver the project. When you have the full picture and a budget constraint emerges, it is then that decisions are made about what has to go. If you discount the plan as you go, you may end up short changing yourself when it comes to budgeting for the resources needed.

Off-site training

In many organisations courses are available either internally or externally to address the needs of the team. Good courses are effective and can increase skill levels quickly—especially if 'just in time' training is done immediately before people need to apply their new skill. These courses are not an opportunity to pass on the responsibility for the training of your people to someone else. It is essential that you set objectives with the person going on the course, making it quite clear why they are going and what you expect from them on their return. The downside is that off-site courses are expensive in money and in time. If this method can be used, select courses carefully.

On the job training

Most individual development takes place on the job. But the trouble with 'on the job' training is that it is often 'on the cheap' training. It can be a euphemism for 'I want to demonstrate my commitment to training but I don't want to spend any time or money on it.' Effective on the job training takes place to a plan for each person with objectives and a means of measurement of progress. Someone has to do it, ensuring that proper dedicated time is allocated to it. This method is effective for most people but it is usually done poorly and instead of improving staff it ends up de-motivating them, as it becomes clear that little actual training is intended. This activity meets the needs of individuals and helps to mould the team as they work with each other—and so relationships grow.

Distance learning and self-study

Distance learning takes the form of a structured course with pre-prepared course materials such as manuals, workbooks, tapes and CD-ROMs used for reference. It is typically done by individuals working on their own with some sort of back up to call on if help is needed. Many of these courses are excellent and are well supported. The difficulty comes in motivating the users to do the work—largely in their own time. Learning styles become a problem because about 25 per cent of people will have preference for learning in this way. This is why most distance learning courses have such a poor completion rate. More than one organisation has spent considerable sums investing in the development of libraries of interactive CD-ROMs dedicated to the subject of project management. They are great for informing people about project management but not necessarily in giving them skills to do the work.

Understandably, organisations which have spent large sums on interactive systems will swear to their effectiveness but many have produced little more than exciting presentations of books with questions. You do not expect people to become proficient at a subject as broad and difficult as project management from books. It is therefore not sensible to expect CD-ROMs to do that much better.

However they are part of the training 'mix' and may be the route that has to be taken. If so then people must be given the opportunity and time to use the system and learn from it.

Coaching

An excellent way of learning is from the personal attention of a coach. Coaching takes place on the job and it aims to increase the skills needed to deliver a task actually being worked on. It is very similar to on the job training but in coaching a specific team member will be given the role of coach to an individual. It goes beyond on the job training because it implies a closer relationship between the coach and the coached. Thus the coaching will go beyond simple skills training and the coach will act as adviser about the formal and informal knowledge that the individual needs. 'How things work around here' guidance. For example, Jill Guido can coach Jim Franz as indeed can Fred Mayes (if he can be persuaded to do it for his own development).

Teaching each other aids team building and if the project manager does some personal coaching, then it supports the leadership role and demonstrates to others that individual development is taken seriously. You can coach individuals or teams as happens in all team sports. The Team Maintenance and Individual Needs circles are nicely addressed by the application of good coaching. Again allocated time is needed and it must be done to a plan. The tasks that are being done whilst coaching is taking place must have a time allocation, or else the task leader will feel undue pressure and the person being coached will not learn.

When you have decided what training activity is wanted for each of your people, enter the information as far as can be seen, onto the implementation plan.

For the brochure project, kick-start the training of the team by sending each of them to an off-site training course. Tasked with building a brochure production capability make sure that you ask for the resources you needed to achieve it. As your people are only working part-time you will need to convince their line managers of the benefits for them.

Jill Guido's competencies are good although she could be stronger in Legal Liaison: you can coach her yourself in that so send her on a project management programme for a week. Fred Mayes needs to boost his brochure design competence—he scores only a three—so he can do a course in that. Jim Franz is fairly new but he will need to develop his technical writing knowledge if he is to be a serious player in the team; he can also do a course.

Step three—staff meetings strategy

You can decide up front what the meetings strategy will be. You need to meet the people as individuals and in teams. Decide in advance how often, where and for how long. Team meetings are expensive in both time and money and the temptation is to try to minimise them but if you do you will jeopardise the forming and functioning of the team—without seeing each other at least occasionally, how can you hope to benefit from team behaviour? Enter team meetings in your implementation plan and publish the dates and times to everyone who needs to know.

Individual meetings
How often are you going to meet team members as individuals? Seeing a person at a meeting does not allow them to meet you as an individual to discuss their needs and wants, hopes and fears for the project and for themselves. So decide beforehand—how often, with whom and for how long?

Social events
It is a good idea to get people together socially—with or without partners. It need not be expensive and can range from an informal evening in the pub or the bowling alley, to a pizza or a fancy dinner when some milestone has been reached. Some older readers may feel that they are past all that but please keep the objective in mind—delivering the project. If team members want to get together out of hours encourage it and contribute financially if you are able. Evenings out help to grow the team by creating a sense of belonging, which can only help in the delivery of the task.

If so, when, where and how often and for how long; will you be buying beer and pizza or something better?

Enter all this in the implementation plan (Figure 5.11), using the following shorthand or one of your own design:

tm—team meeting
pm—project management training
s—social outing
tw—technical writing training

i—individual meeting
c—coaching followed by subject
bd—brochure design training

Cautionary note

For the purposes of learning concepts a deliberately simple but realistic example is used here. If you expand the length of this ten week project to say six months and to double the number of people involved to six, then the importance of this level of planning becomes crucial to the success of the project.

From those parameters the following can be calculated:

- Team meetings: say 1 per week lasting an average of 2 hours. Therefore 7 people (includes you) × 2 hrs × 26 weeks = 364 hours.
- Individual meetings: say an average of 1 per month per person lasting 1.5 hrs. Therefore 6 people × 3 hrs (includes you) × 6 months = 108 hours.
- Training and development: say average of 2 days per person during project. Therefore 6 people × 15 hrs + 50 per cent for coaches' time = 135 hours.
- Task briefings: 30 tasks needing say an average of 1 hour brief and discussion. Therefore 30 tasks × 2 people average (plus you) × 1 hour = 90 hours.
  Total time = 697 hours.
  Or, taking a 10 hour working day = *70 days.*

TEAM	Week Number	1	2	3	4	5	6	7	8	9	10
Name: **Guido**	Do task letter	A	B	B	E	E	E	F			H
BD CW PG TW LL FP PL 7 7 9 6 5 6 9	Training and meetings	tm	i	tm		tm	s		pm	c,ll	s
Name: **Mayes**	Do task letter	A	C	C	E	E	E		G	G	
BD CW PG TW LL FP PL 3 4 8 5 8 6 6	Training and meetings	tm	i	tm		tm	s	i		bd	s
Name: **Franz**	Do task letter	A		D	D	D	D		G		
BD CW PG TW LL FP PL 2 3 7 0 8 0 4	Training and meetings	tm	tw	i, tm		tm	s	i			s

Figure 5.11   Implementation plan—training and meetings added

This figure of 70 days represents 14 five-day weeks for one person. Yet many projects are launched without regard to the cost of these activities—project managers think that somehow these things will be 'fitted in'. So you start to see why nights and weekends are worked just to keep up to schedule—this is also why some schedules simply cannot work within the constraints of inadequate planning.

Summary

Leadership takes time and commitment. In comparison with task planning the leadership of people is an act of faith—it does not always work and the link between the activity and the output is often tenuous. However, omitting leadership from the plans will ensure that leadership will only happen by accident rather than design. If you don't plan for it and cost it, then it will not appear in the Defensible Plan. Consider the people as individuals and as members of teams and address both separately. Not planning for meetings means that the project is under resourced so you will stress yourself and the project team members trying to 'make time' for unplanned meetings which must take place.

The implementation plan is filling up but you are not yet finished. You need to think about some insurance to cover you against *risk*, the subject of the next chapter.

Managing risk

*If a little knowledge is dangerous, where is the man who has so much
as to be out of danger?*
T. H. Huxley *On Elementary Instruction in Physiology* (1877)

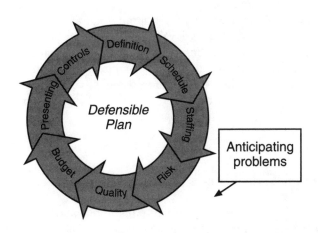

Introduction

Projects by their very nature are risky undertakings. They are unique,
they don't get repeated, they need all the skills of the general manager
and they need lots of intelligent guesswork when estimating time and
resources and so on. And more projects fail than succeed!

But human lives are full of risk. Every day when we step out of our
front door we expose our frail human bodies to danger and we can't
even bear to think about the dangers to which our children are constantly exposed. Yet most survive—and we survive because we do our
best to control or eliminate the risks we take in our daily lives.

The popularity of dangerous sports is increasing. Sky diving, parachuting, hang gliding, pot holing, mountaineering and of course bungee
jumping—yet participants do not wish to die. Those who are going to
do something as illogical as jumping from a perfectly serviceable
aircraft, are concerned about how safe parachuting actually is. They
want to be reassured of the *safety in the danger*. If falling too fast,

parachutists now have reserve parachutes that are automatically opened by barometric pressure control at low altitude. These remove the risk of the unconscious parachutist falling to the ground, being unable to pull a reserve after mid air collision with other free-fallers. Climbers are constantly developing stronger and more efficient cara-biners to catch them should they fall, thereby reducing the risk of injury or death. Sub-aqua divers have developed sophisticated pro-cedures that are drilled into novices in order to reduce the risks of misunderstood communications. We protect ourselves from damage in risk situations all the time.

In project management there are a number of issues that can be addressed when considering risk. You can try to *prevent* the unwanted happening. You can use *controls* to give early warning that the unwanted is happening or is about to happen. You can plan *contingency* actions to be taken when the unwanted event actually happens. But before you do any of these you must identify those things that can go wrong on the project.

Identify the risks

Identify the risks in your plans by thinking about and writing down all the things that could go wrong. If you walk through your implementa-tion plan you will be able to identify and write down the possible points of weakness or vulnerability. It also helps if you can mentally 'grow' the problem, taking a problem through to its ultimate result. You should keep asking yourself 'What will this mean for the project?' It is not a happy process to mentally think about your project falling about your ears but it is essential in understanding what could go wrong. If you can't see what could go wrong then you will be unable to plan for the result.

Using the brochure example, could:

- you lose a member of the team?
- your photographer let you down?
- tasks overrun if necessary?
- the people you want to join the project be available at the time when you want them to join?
- the product specification change halfway through?
- you, as project manager, be pulled away to do other work?
- work be added to the project after it has begun?
- you cope if Fred Mayes doesn't cooperate with Jill Guido?
- you accept budget cuts?
- the competencies of the team fail to improve?

Talking to other people in your organisation who have been doing similar projects can help you identify things that can go wrong.

Understand the impact

Having identified the risks, you need to understand their impact. How hard will the project be hit?

Number the risks identified and then sort them into two categories: high impact and low impact.

Number	Risk	Impact on Project
1	Lose a member of the project team	High
2	Photographer doesn't deliver	High
3	Tasks overrun	Low
4	Team members not available	High
5	Change of product specification	Low
6	Project manager (you) pulled away	High
7	New work added after start	High
8	Fred Mayes doesn't cooperate	Low
9	Budget cut	High
10	No change in team competencies	High
11	Lawyer is late with clearance	High
12	Printer not ready	Low
13	etc	

There are more risks to be considered but for the purposes of illustration let's stop there.

Assess risk probability

You must now assess the likelihood or probability of the event happening. Again, use high and low impact categories. This assessment is about knowing your organisation's culture and typical occurrences. Thinking that these things will not happen to you is not good planning for risk. For example, if people continuously get pulled away from projects in your organisation then you must plan for it happening to you. If it does happen you may have a perfect excuse for your project not delivering but you will have failed to be *effective* and organisations want effective project managers, not failed project managers with lots of mitigation as to why they failed.

So, do your homework and decide on probability.

Number	Risk	Impact on Project	Probability
1	Lose a member of the project team	High	High
2	Photographer doesn't deliver	High	Low
3	Tasks overrun	Low	High
4	Team members not available	High	Low
5	Change of product specification	Low	High
6	Project manager (you) pulled away	High	Low
7	New work added after start	High	High
8	Fred Mayes doesn't cooperate	Low	Low
9	Budget cut	High	Low
10	No change in team competencies	High	Low
11	Lawyer is late with clearance	High	Low
12	Printer not ready	Low	High
13	etc.		

Plot a risk matrix

Take each of your risks and plot them on as an impact/probability matrix (Figure 6.1).

High Probability, Low Impact	High Probability, High Impact
3 Tasks overrun 5 Change of product specification 12 Printer not ready	1 Lose a member of the project team 7 New work added after start
Low Probability, Low Impact	**Low Probability, High Impact**
8 Fred Mayes doesn't cooperate	2 Photographer doesn't deliver 4 Team members not available 6 Project manager (you) pulled away 9 Budget cut 10 No change in team competencies 11 Lawyer is late with clearance

Figure 6.1   Impact/probability matrix

Decide your risk management strategy

Having identified what the risks are and how likely they are to occur decide what to do about them. It is possible to insure against most occurrences but there is a point where the cost of cover outweighs its benefits. Therefore, compromise between risk, the cost of covering the risk and the acceptability of the risk that remains uncovered. The choices to be made are similar to those in your personal life: you can do nothing and hope for the best; you can prevent the risk happening; or you can apply some control system or contingency plan to adopt should the risk occur. The implications of each of these are:

- Do nothing: be willing to live with the consequences of the event happening.
- Prevent the risk: stop the event occurring. This approach is about thinking ahead of events and preventing the unwanted happening. This needs you to be in proactive mode as opposed to reactive. Getting agreement from the boss that Guido will not be taken away from your project for any reason is an example. You could plan for the event happening but how much better it is to prevent it happening in the first place. To be properly cautious you would do both.
- Use controls: ensure that the right control procedures are in place to give early warning that the event could occur and reduce the impact. For example, correct control of the critical path will tell you if the project is about to go over schedule so that you can then adopt your contingency plan to bring the schedule back on track.
- Use contingency: plan actions to be taken when the event occurs to reduce the impact of the risk. For example, having someone with the right skills and competencies standing by ready to take over from Jill Guido if she becomes ill.

Go back to your risk matrix and apply an initial 'blanket' decision to each of the quadrants and produce an updated impact/probability matrix (Figure 6.2).

High Probability, Low Impact	High Probability, High Impact
Contingency Plan	*Prevent these Occurring*
3 Tasks overrun	1 Lose a member of the project team
5 Change of product specification	7 New work added after start
12 Printer not ready	
Low Probability, Low Impact	**Low Probability, High Impact**
Do Nothing	*Control for Early Warning*
8 Fred Mayes doesn't cooperate	2 Photographer doesn't deliver
	4 Team members not available
	6 Project manager (you) pulled away
	9 Budget cut
	10 No change in team competencies
	11 Lawyer is late with clearance

Figure 6.2   Updated impact/probability matrix

Low impact and low probability

For low impact and low probability, risk 8 in Figure 6.2, decide to *do nothing* and accept that should this risk occur, it will need no out of the ordinary action from you. Of course, if Fred Mayes does not cooperate you will have to manage the situation but it does not jeopardise your project delivery.

High impact and high probability

For high impact and high probability, risks 1 and 7, *prevent* the threat occurring if you possibly can. In the example, there is a high probability key people will be pulled away and that the impact will be high (risk 1). To prevent this happening obtain from your boss, in advance, agreement that this will not happen. But to ensure that you can defend your plan you also plan a contingency in case it does happen. Bosses can give reassurances that they will not take people away and they honestly mean it at the time. However, the situation can change and they may be left with no choice but to break their 'promises'. Machiavelli told us 'to never trust a prince—they will always plead expediency'. Unfair but true. To ensure that you deliver your projects you will address 'prevention' risks but you will also plan a contingency just in case. This is good insurance. If you smash your car you want to know that your insurance will repair it. However, if you use your car for work, you will also insure yourself to be given another car when your own is in the repair shop.

In the brochure example, there are different actions for different people so contingency actions will number more than one. Jill Guido being pulled away will have far greater impact than losing Jim Franz, so differing contingencies will be needed for each. They needn't be long but they do need to be considered. Because she is pivotal to the project, Jill Guido being pulled away will need a swift contingency plan. Either identify someone internally to replace her and get agreement that they will be made available immediately, or employ an external consultant to take over the work. Alternatively, another member of the team could be trained to replace Jill Guido. For risks that are high impact and high probability, options are likely to be expensive so they will need to be budgeted for. That is why they are planned for now, before costs are worked out.

Low impact and high probability

For low impact and high probability, risks 3, 5 and 12, plan *contingencies*—plans for actions to be taken when the risk actually happens. With risk 3—activities running over time—plan what you will do when this happens as it is a common occurrence in projects. What is done will differ from task to task and those on the critical path will need tighter contingency over those with slack. The same goes for tasks that precede outside contractor tasks. Contractors may not be able to accept late delivery. They too have a work schedule and a small delay can lose you your production 'slot' unless you negotiate some slack in advance from suppliers. Overtime can be allocated or you can put more people on the task if this makes sense. You can also take up slack if the task is not on the critical path.

High impact and low probability

For high impact and low probability risks, ensure that the right *controls* are in place to give early warning that the risk is likely to occur. The fact that these threats are of low probability means that you can fail to look for them and then you are caught napping. You need to be alert. (Later in the book you will be looking closely at controls to help you implement projects.)

However, for risk 4, you might consider it unlikely that Jill Guido is not available but you have to force yourself to consider the consequences if she is not, and decide what the early warning signs might be. For example, I lost a key worker who was a very happy and effective member of my team. He left when his wife was made an offer she couldn't refuse and they decided that he should move jobs to be with her. The best of reasons but inconvenient and in need of a contingency plan.

For risk 2, we might know and trust our photographers but they could for example, have a fire on their site through no fault of their own which could then leave us high and dry without photography. To succeed, plan for all eventualities. In the example, are alternative suppliers identified and do we know their supply times? Do we know how much it will cost to commission another photographer? What are the photographers' contingency plans for the unforeseen—have *their* contingency plans been seen?

Having decided what the contingencies are, make shorthand notes on the implementation plan to remind you what you have decided to do should particular situations arise.

We now turn our attention to delivering quality on projects.

Delighting customers

'To found a great empire for the sole purpose of raising up a people of customers, may at first sight appear a project fit only for a nation of shopkeepers. It is however, a project altogether unfit for a nation of shopkeepers; but extremely fit for a nation whose government is influenced by shopkeepers.'
Adam Smith (1723–1790) *The Wealth of Nations*

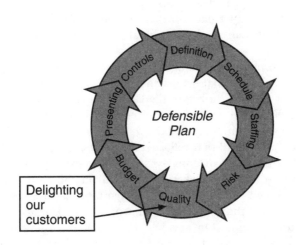

Adam Smith would not be surprised at either the influence of business and trade on governments of today nor at the influence of customers on shopkeepers. As shopkeeper, project managers have customers to serve and are in the business of securing customers through total satisfaction and delight. This may seem obvious when dealing with external customers (who produce revenue) but not so much for internal customers.

We hear a lot about delighting our customers but what exactly does it mean? What is the difference between satisfying a customer and delighting them? Here is an example.

For many years I drove a specific make of car — one that dominated a part of the market which considered safety a major buying concern. The car's safety features contributed to the saving of the life of one of my sales managers, during a particularly nasty accident. As a result this manufacturer's cars became the choice of myself and all my managers.

I then bought another car, the same make, for the family (including our au pair who helped look after our little girls). Intermittently, the car refused to start. Each time the dealership took it back promising faithfully that they would fix it this time. The final straw came when my children were for the third time stranded quite a way from home and their recovery became a major operation. In frustration I tracked down the previous owner of the car from the vehicle registration documents and in a short conversation it became clear that I had been sold a 'problem' car that had been returned to the dealership. On challenging the sales manager of the dealership he admitted that the car had 'a history' but he said that he honestly believed his mechanics had found the problem. But why test their solutions on my children? Why couldn't the mechanic take the car home until he was absolutely sure he had fixed the problem? The dealership replaced the car and did their best to make amends but trust had gone. After driving this marque for twelve years, poor quality in a relatively small matter drove me away, I felt I had little choice.

I then did something I thought I would never do. I went to look at BMW. My view was that whilst the BMW car is a beautiful piece of engineering it was overpriced in the UK. On arrival at the showroom, I was well received and dealt with courteously by the sales team.

I entered into negotiation and the discussion was open, fair and realistic and reached a deal that reflected the most competitive rates I could get anywhere in the finance markets. I bought the car and arranged to collect it the following weekend. I arrived on the Saturday and was thoroughly shown round the car and taken for a drive. I was a satisfied customer. I signed the necessary documentation and returned to the car and then drove home. On parking, I noticed something on the back seat—it was a bottle of champagne complete with ribbons and a card saying 'Mr & Mrs Webster please enjoy your BMW driving experience'. How did I feel? I was delighted. The showroom had considered me as a person and took the trouble to include my wife who was also going to drive the car. I had just spent thousands of pounds for the car and all that it took to delight me was a £20 bottle of champagne!

Delighting is not about cost it is about action—appropriate action. If the BMW dealership had given me a case of champagne, I would have been concerned about the extra costs that I was paying for in the price of the car. Having delighted me once, they keep on reinforcing the delight every time I make contact. I know I am paying for it but I don't mind because my perception of the value is high. It is going to be hard to get me out of a BMW.

Building quality into the process

Delivering quality is not easy and it cannot be delivered unless the operational part of the project itself is right. Delivering quality from a base of inadequate planning is an impossibility—a good customer will feel manipulated if the operation goes wrong and the project manager seems unable to put matters right—regardless of how well he or she is treated. So quality must enter at the very start of a project.

You will be pleased to know that your plan has had quality built in from the beginning. Building in quality means using quality tools from the outset—no compromise on quality for any reason. The tools that you have been using are quality tools to give quality output. Quality means doing it right first time. It is the direct result of everything done in planning and executing the project until the results are acceptable to the customer and consistent with the company strategy for customer satisfaction.

As with all parts of preparing for project implementation you need a plan (Figure 7.1).

☑ **Project Definition**

■ Deliverables
■ Requirements
■ Specifications

☑ **Work Break Down Structure**

Identify what has to be done

Break-down work to activities that are clear, have specific deliverables, and include quality metrics

■ Include testing/integrating/proofing type of activities
■ Specify competencies required

☑ **Match People to Activities**

☑ **Schedule of Project Team Meetings and other individual and team development activities**

☐ Schedule of Task reviews

☐ Schedule of Project reviews

☐ Schedule of Supplier reviews

Figure 7.1   Components of a quality plan: the parts

In Figure 7.1 the last three schedules of task, project and supplier reviews remain to be done. The first two are concerned with your customer; the third concerns yourself as a customer of your suppliers. We will address these later.

Customers

Your customers are those for whom you are delivering the project. It matters not whether they are internal or external, they would like to be delighted in the same way. Organisations that delight their external customers have a high regard for their internal customers. It is hard to treat customers like kings if you are being treated like a slave. All those affected by your project should hold you in high regard and this is achieved by delighting them in the delivery process. Ensure that you understand who the 'stakeholders' are in your project. They are all those people who will be impacted by the project itself—not just those directly involved but all those who need to know that the project is happening. It can be a wide network of people. Purchasing, human resources, design, administration, sales and marketing and so on. If in doubt, tell them what you are doing. It is better to risk too much communication than to miss out an important stakeholder.

In the brochure project the stakeholders include all those already involved in the project as well as those who will use the brochure. The sales managers, their sales people, promotions, technical sales are all stakeholders and in this case they are your customers too. These are the people you need to delight so that they ask you to produce the next brochure for them.

This delight has become most important in many organisations where outsourcing is permitted. If internal suppliers do not do the job to the quality, price, schedule *and delight* of their internal customers then these customers are free to acquire what they need from any source they choose. In some organisations this has seen whole departments close down when those in charge of them have been unable to produce the improvements demanded by internal customers.

In the case of the brochure it is policy for the moment that brochures are produced internally. It is a matter of the ability and determination of the selected project manager whether it is done to the delight of customers or not. Success for the project manager will lead to recognition, possibly reward, but most certainly more responsibility. For the ambitious (the reader of this book is likely to be ambitious—at least wants to do a better job) having a reputation as a successful deliverer of quality projects is an aim worth pursuing.

Quality product and delivery

Your customers consider two dimensions when thinking about quality: the outcome of the project itself and how that outcome was achieved. In other words '*What* did they get and *how* did they get it? There are plenty of examples where project managers delivered what was expected but the customer was dissatisfied. If how the project was delivered did not please the customer, the project manager will not be welcome again—even though the project itself was on time, to cost and to specification. How your customer gets the project is wrapped up in a *psychological contract* that exists between the project manager and the customer.

The psychological contract

The psychological contract is all about expectation—what your customer expects of you and what you expect of your customer. The term comes from the world of employment where it is used to describe the expectations of the employee and the employer. Carole Pemberton, in her book *Strike a New Career Deal* (Pitman Publishing, 1995) defines it thus:

'The psychological contract is the exchange deal which the individual and the organisation believes it has with each other'

Most of us have formal employment contracts that are required by law. Even though each 'i' is dotted and each 't' is crossed it is virtually impossible to write down all elements of an employment contract—there are expectations of both parties that are understood or are 'psychological' and are not written down. Although they exist only in the corporate mind of the employer and in the mind of the employee, expectations are the source of much discontent between organisations and their staff. A significant psychological contract exists between you as project manager and the people who will work with you. Both have expectations that are not written down anywhere but the differences in these expectations can create much discontent. Here is an example.

A friend of mine, on taking on a new job with a consulting firm, experienced differing expectations:

He expected ...	The organisation expected ...
to be well treated and respected as having potential to grow in the organisation.	to get as much as possible out of eager new employees.

to bring his previous experience to bear in changing the organisation.	him to be inducted into the company way, so that he was quickly shaped by the organisation
a period of time to settle in without earning for the organisation.	him to earn his costs from day one.
to influence the work he did and how he did it.	him to do as he was told.
to work so that he could spend time with his family and pursue outside interests.	total commitment to the exclusion of his personal life.

From this example it can be seen that there was high potential for discontent as the discrepancies between expectancies were uncovered as time passed. My friend left the organisation within a year. These psychological understandings have nothing to do with the formal or written contract, they exist to one side of things formal. Each party can be meticulous in meeting the demands of the formal agreement but still be at each other's throats over the psychological contract.

There exists a similar psychological contract between you and the customers of your projects. These are the things you cannot write down—the expectations that each of you has of the other. And, like the employment contract, there is plenty of room for misunderstanding if there is not enough contact between the contract holders early enough in the planning process. It is here that you might glimpse the difference between satisfaction and delight.

Satisfaction and delight

If you deliver your project exactly as given in the project definition you will, at best, satisfy your customer. To delight them you must also satisfy the unwritten psychological contract. It could read something like this:

As project manager I expect . . .	**As customer I expect . . .**
all changes to specifications will be freshly resourced in full.	some tolerances over specification changes as no-one can see all the needs of a project at the beginning.
customers to be on call to help me.	I will have some notice of meetings.

customers to add their delays to the time schedule.	the project manager will absorb delays and deliver on time even if the project overruns.
tolerance over activity delays beyond my control.	there is nothing beyond the project manager's control.
I will report on the project status at formal presentations only.	I can have impromptu updates whenever I want.

In the two lists above you can see the possibility of conflict is present because expectations in some areas are far apart.

Not a penny more . . .

I am currently working with an organisation which vehemently insists on the delivery of the project contract. 'Not one penny more' is indelibly stamped on the foreheads of the organisation's project managers who are ever alert to being taken advantage of by their nasty customers. They wonder why they are constantly at odds with their clients—why they deliver good projects but are never invited back. They win business where their expertise is unique but they are not invited for the general business which would help them grow into other sectors.

Looking back into the history of this organisation I found what I expected, a manager who, at some point, lost out (his own perception) to a client. Specifications may have grown out of hand without protection in a contract; or some misunderstanding led to unacceptable cost or time overrun. The manager blames the client (it takes a great deal of maturity to blame oneself) and makes sure that it cannot happen again. This is done by laying down absolutes with no room for manoeuvre by people at the coal face. In business, as in life, extremes of anything are probably not a good idea.

Behaviour like this is simply opting out, thereby putting customer delight into the 'too difficult' basket by hiding behind overly simplistic rules and procedures. Delighting customers is difficult because it is an emotional thing, away from balance sheets and work breakdown structures—it deals with imperfect and inconsistent human beings. But in delighting your customers—that is where you must go. Effective project managers deliver the project specification—*what*—and they also meet the expectations of the customer's psychological contract—*how*.

If you say that a satisfied customer has 100 per cent of the project delivered, then you can say that delighting the customer takes place above that functional 100 per cent and moves into the personal and the emotional (Figure 7.2).

It is most unlikely that you will delight a customer functionally delivering

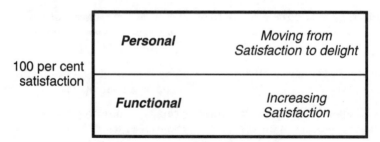

Figure 7.2   Satisfaction levels

your projects. To delight, you must look at the needs of the person and do your best to meet them even though they may not be explicit. Finding out what may be in the minds of your customers needs you to have a good relationship with them. Without good relationships it is difficult to find out anything worthwhile.

Quality standards

Many project management organisations have taken considerable trouble to acquire international standards in recognition of their project management and in the hope that their quality will improve. There is no doubt that formal standards contribute to quality but they have more to do with quality *procedures* than with quality *process*. ISO is an example of the 'guardian' type of quality that ensures that an organisation efficiently follows its own quality procedures. Such standards tend to be bureaucratic concentrating on the following of a procedure based system. By themselves they won't deliver quality as many organisations have found out. The delivery of these standards alone will not mean delighted or even satisfied customers. The emotional needs as well as the functional needs of the customer have to be satisfied. To do one without the other might bring satisfaction but it will not bring them delight.

Delighting the customer means delivering the project the way the customer wants it delivered, not how you think it should be delivered—even when you know best. Your customer will tell you how they want it done if you give them the opportunity to do so. That opportunity comes from being in regular contact so that you can grow relationships with your customers to enable them to communicate well with you.

Relationships

I have a business relationship with my hairdresser in the town where I live. Although he is in his forties, he seems to spend his life with people considerably younger than himself. His shop is in the middle of the town and it serves the community as the centre of gossip (male and female) about anything worthwhile that is happening with the 'in crowd'. He is also a very competent barber who knows immediately if I have exposed my head to the shears of a competitor.

I was at his shop 'first thing' one morning and, as always, laughed at his window sign which states that he opens at '10ish'. It was now 10.35 and there was no sign of him as I waited with my daughter who was keeping me company. The postman went past and, smiling, commented on the hairdresser's usual lateness. The hairdresser eventually showed up at 10.45 full of apology. He immediately opened up a conversation with my 12-year-old daughter and had her at ease in minutes. He carried on a conversation with me practically where we had left off six weeks earlier. He cuts hair at a leisurely pace, giving his customers the feeling that he is doing things properly. He uses small scissors and there is hardly an electric tool in sight. He is always busy even though he has plenty of competitors all around him.

He forms good relationships with his customers, he remembers who they are and how they like to have their hair cut. There is always something going on in his shop and he is a mine of information about anything happening in the town. He tries out the new restaurants and is not afraid to make recommendations.

The result of all this attention is that he is readily forgiven his shortcomings and idiosyncrasies. He is forgiven for always been late because he treats you as more than simply his customers and he demands to be treated as more than a hairdresser.

On your projects, if good relationships can be formed with customers, then you too will be forgiven your shortcomings and your idiosyncrasies provided you are genuine about what you do for your customers. If things go wrong you will be given more leeway than your brethren who do not attempt to grow relationships with their customers.

The opposite is also true. If you do not have good relationships, when things go wrong they tend to get worse; the relationship deteriorates further until you can do nothing right and the customer is positively looking for reason to find fault.

Regular contact

Relationships cannot form without human contact. Customer relationships are no different from any other relationship. Without quality contact they will fade and die. There must also be regular contact as the relationships you 'have in the bank' will lose their value if the principal investment is not looked after. In your personal lives, there is little point in spending a fortune on dinners and shows at the beginning of a new relationship and then disappearing for three months. The previous investment is lost if continuous contact is not maintained. At best you will have to start again, at worst the competition will have taken over!

So it is with your project management relationships. To have any chance of delighting your customers you must meet with them often. Then you are available to discuss the project with them and to put right immediately any concerns that may be manifesting themselves.

It is a simple action but an important one if you are to grow relationships—resolve to meet your customers often. You never hear of staff complaining about too much feedback from their bosses; similarly, you never hear of customers having too much access to their suppliers!

Measuring quality

Just like any other area of business, measure your quality performance. This can be done in a number of ways but keep it simple. For some projects you might measure the failure rate of a component against an industry standard—good quality measurement refers to external as well as internal measurement. There is little use being top internally when the whole organisation is bottom externally.

For IT projects the measure could be bugs per line of code. For welding how many poor welds per 100 feet of pipe. For service industries you can measure complaints and commendations (letters or calls made by customers to praise staff on the project).

The important part of the quality process is to define what is meant by good quality in the eyes of the customer. What is important to them? Then measure it using some tangible method which makes it visible. Then deliver it and in the process delight your customers.

The brochure project will measure *enhancements*.

Enhancements

As projects are implemented, additional work will emerge that no one thought of during the planning stage. This additional work, or *enhance-*

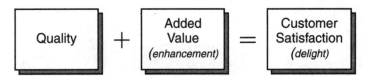

Figure 7.3   Enhancements

ments, may include improvements or changes that could be done as the project is implemented: a small change here, an addition there, a better way of doing something that emerges midway through a task. These enhancements are not about changes of specification or significant additional work. They are the little actions, for example the unexpected bottle of champagne, or the unexpected 'no charge sir' (Figure 7.3).

Delight is about adding value through enhancing the project delivery to the delight of the customer. Here is an example.

My wife wanted the kitchen remodelled and electrical power points were a matter of discussion. We decided the number and positions and briefed our builder about what was wanted. When he did the work he added two electrical points above a worktop that we had not asked for. He told us that we would need them to power kitchen tools. He was absolutely right. He knew and we didn't, so he gave us the best advice and the two sockets at no extra charge—he did the enhancement as he was making his way through his project plan. We were delighted.

There are two types of enhancements: the ones the customer asks for and the ones that you and your people know are needed from experience. They need not cost much but doing both shows that you are constantly thinking of your customers as the job gets done. This is how to contribute to their delight.

Review meetings

Earlier in this chapter the components of a Quality Plan were outlined. There were three schedules of review meetings that remained to be done; they were task, project and suppliers. Delighting your customers cannot be done entirely for nothing. If you want to delight your customers you will have to meet with them, as indeed will your staff. If you meet and listen to them, then you will pick up the changes they would like to see as the tasks are carried out. These meetings are *task* reviews. As project manager you can meet with the person who will agree that the whole project has been done. Additionally, your people might be working with internal customers who will confirm that parts of the project are being delivered as needed, so face-to-face meetings should

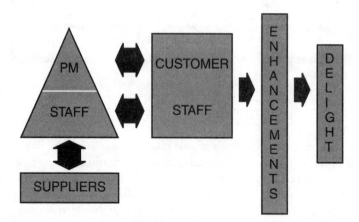

Figure 7.4   Quality reviews

happen between your people and the customer's staff at that level too. These are *project* reviews.

These review meetings give your customers the opportunity to feed back to you how they feel the project is going. It also gives them the opportunity to ask for enhancements that they have identified. Any enhancements emerging should be done quickly or they will become a complaint—you raised expectation of high quality so you must meet the expectation. It is more cost effective to do enhancements as you go along rather than send people back to do them later.

In turn, if you have suppliers, you should press them for their schedule of review meetings including what they will do about enhancements (Figure 7.4). These are *supplier* reviews.

As project manager you will meet the customer and your staff will meet with the customer's staff. From these meetings you would expect enhancements to emerge. Timely completion of these enhancements will delight your customer. Finally, you should expect your suppliers to carry out enhancements for you in their quality plan.

Project reviews

Project reviews are the meetings you as project manager hold with the project specifier to review the project as a whole. They will not happen often but you must remember to book space in the specifier's diary. For the brochure example you might need to meet three times: one month into the project, again at two months, and once more at the end.

Task reviews

Jill Guido, Fred Mayes and Jim Franz who are controlling tasks will meet with those doing the tasks to ensure that they are getting what they want. When photographic proofs of the product are ready (task D) they will be inspected by Jim Franz and then shown to the customer who will choose the most suitable images. If this choice was made without the customer's agreement then he or she may be less than delighted with the choice. At this stage they may ask for a different image presentation of the product to illustrate a particular feature that is hidden in the photographs already taken.

The more reviews that are done, the sooner enhancements will be identified and entered into the work flow and the greater the chance of customer delight. As project manager you can make a strategic decision about the frequency of reviews and communicate it to your people. You can ask for reviews at the end of activities, in addition to halfway through; or every third or quarter completion, depending on the length of the task. A one week task will likely have only one review at the end, two weeks might have one in the middle of the task and another at the end. A four or five week task will have more. You make your decisions, communicate them to your teams and add the schedule to your implementation plan.

Supplier meetings

Supplier reviews are as important as your customer reviews. Too many project managers who have failed to deliver their projects readily blame poor suppliers. It may be that they were let down but who is in charge of the project? It is the job of the project manager to deliver the project. A failed project with justifiable mitigation is still a failed project. It is better that you join the ranks of the successful project manager than to join the ranks of the failed—but with good excuses. You should understand the capabilities of your suppliers, plan for that capability and ensure that you get what has been agreed. To know what is going on with suppliers treat them the same as other people in your teams who are delivering important parts of the project—meet them, grow relationships with them, agree a contact strategy and stick to it. It is worth meeting them long before reaching the time they start to work for you. This gives you the opportunity to brief them on the task to be done and alerts them to the fact that you are keen and interested and that you have expectations that are to be met. Decide what you are to do and then enter your decisions in your implementation plan.

Cost of delight

Having worked out your strategy you can add up the number of meetings and their cost. The costs of enhancements are more elusive. In the absence of any enhancement information an allowance of between 5 and 10 per cent of budget can be used. Less than 5 per cent is unlikely to bring delight. More than 10 per cent would indicate that either specification changes or rework is being accommodated and some additional charges would be appropriate. This allowance needs to be added to your budget. The omission of such an allowance sees project managers unable to entertain the most meagre of enhancement requests and thus the relationships they have with their customers is likely to deteriorate.

Let's return to the implementation plan for the brochure. How often will the team meet to discuss the project's progress? What are the instructions to Jill Guido, Fred Mayes and Jim Franz about task reviews

TEAM	Week Number	1	2	3	4	5	6	7	8	9	10
Name: **Guido**	Do task letter	A	B	B	E	E	E	F			H
BD CW PG TW LL FP PL 7 7 9 6 5 6 9	Training and meetings	tm	i	tm		tm	s		pm	c,ll	s
Review task... ...			a	b		e		e			h
Name: **Mayes**	Do task letter	A	C	C	E	E	E		G	G	
BD CW PG TW LL FP PL 3 4 8 5 8 6 6	Training and meetings	tm	i	tm		tm	s	i		bd	s
Review task... ...			a	c		e		e		g	g
Name: **Franz**	Do task letter	A		D	D	D	D		G		
BD CW PG TW LL FP PL 2 3 7 0 8 0 4	Training and meetings	tm	tw	i, tm		tm	s	i			s
Review task... ...					d			d			
PM to review supplier for task...			d				f		h		
Project review by PM					✓			✓			✓

Figure 7.5   Implementation plan: task, project and supplier reviews added

and how often do you want them? What are they to do about enhancements when they arise? How much should be allowed for in the budget for enhancements to be done? The lower the skills the more enhancements will be asked for by the customer who will find improvements that better able people would have made as they went along. Each enhancement will be an average of about three hours' work. Allowing 10 per cent for enhancements, a 10 week project will use up a week in unseen work which means that the plan needs to cater for about 12 enhancements to be done; or one per project week.

Enter your decisions in the implementation plan (Figure 7.5).

The project manager is getting involved with meeting key suppliers and also in ensuring that the project sponsor is kept informed—again through meetings.

The Defensible Plan is almost complete. How much is it all going to cost? That brings us to the budget, the subject of the next chapter.

Building a budget

'He told me the other day that it was provided for. That was Mr
Micawber's expression, "Provided for".'
Charles Dickens (1812–1870) *David Copperfield*

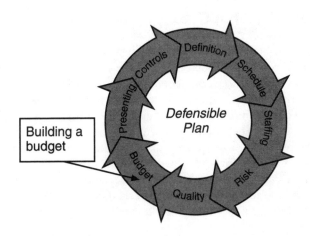

The Defensible Plan ensures that everything needed is budgeted and
'provided for'. Projects' budgets run adrift when halfway through implementation it is found that needed resources have not been budgeted for.

A dictionary definition of 'budgeting' is 'a translation of all resources
needed into monetary terms'. This description is rather arid. Looking at
your personal life you will find that you spend most of your money on
things you consider important. If you want to assess the personal priorities of an individual look at what they do with their money. If there is
a match between what they consider important in their lives, and on what
they spend their money, there is coherence. An individual who espouses
family security will have plenty of life assurance, personal health cover, a
well composed will and financial plans for schooling, universities and
pensions; everything to do with family security is 'provided for'.

If that same person lives in rented accommodation, is without life
insurance or financial plans for the future; drives a new, upmarket
sports car which is changed each year, wears designer suits, watches
and shoes and belongs to the best exclusive country clubs, then there is
a lack of coherence; what is said and what is done are two different

things. In modern parlance, the lips and feet are not moving in the same direction.

So it is with project budgets. Look at how money is allocated on a project and you will have a good idea of the values and priorities of the project manager. Therefore, the budgetary process can be livened up by seeing it as more than just 'a translation of all resources needed into monetary terms'. Ensure that what is important to you as a project manager is reflected in how you spend money.

Deciding priorities

When rolling out your project you will give team members your priorities for the project. That is, priorities regarding schedule, cost, quality and human resources (people).

These priorities are essential for the decision-making of team members. They need to know the order of these priorities which cannot all be equal even if they are all important. For example, when behind on an activity is the team to spend money to catch up? Which has greater priority—the budget or the schedule? The same goes for the other options. In a budget you should see coherence between stated priorities and how the money is to be spent. If schedule is the first priority then there should be a budget allocation for overtime working or additional help.

If quality is the first priority, then there will be plenty of customer review meetings at various levels in the project to extract enhancements and time allowed for them. It doesn't mean that a lower priority sees no money; it does mean that the order of project management's values and priorities will be reflected in the allocation of budget.

'Finger in the air' budgeting

All too often, projects are initiated with a budgeted figure already stated for their delivery. Unless there is some evidence of the detailed work needed to produce an accurate budget you should ignore any 'finger in the air' budgets and start with a blank sheet of paper.

For example, having done some detailed planning, you have a reasonable picture of the project. You also know what is needed to do it well. You build your Defensible Plan from a 'perfect world' point of view. As it grows you give yourself anything and everything you require to deliver your perfect project plan. You know that you are unlikely to get all of it but if you don't know what the project needs in its entirety, then you will have little idea by how much you have restricted yourself when you present your Defensible Plan. When you ask for the resources you need, you can indicate, first, what is needed and, second, what voluntary restrictions you have assumed in reaching the finished plan. If you never grow the total extent of the project's dimensions, you will never 'see' what it is that you really need to deliver the perfect project.

Start with a blank sheet of paper and build up the budget from the implementation plan including schedule, risk, leadership and quality plans. You do not live in a perfect world and you will not be given all the resources you need all the time, but by building the picture of the total project you will be better able to understand and deal with the impact of any resource reductions imposed.

Project controls

Without an agreed budget you will not be able to build a decent set of project controls. Controls are there to tell you how well you are doing against the set of standards you have laid down. Many of those standards emanate from the budgetary process so without a budget it becomes more difficult to deliver your projects under some sort of control. Using the brochure example a Defensible Plan can be built in a number of steps.

Step 1—calculate task and quality hours

Task hours are those directly concerned only with the delivery of tasks. They do not include briefings, meetings, training or anything else that is not concerned with actual working on tasks. They do include the time set aside for doing quality work (enhancements). This is done by going to the implementation plan and physically counting all the weeks where people are working on tasks. That total is multiplied by the number of hours people are available in a working week.

For producing the brochure, given a situation of previous poor quality, customer satisfaction has to be the highest priority so it makes sense to add additional task hours for the completion of enhancements during project implementation—say, 10 per cent.

We update our implementation plan with this information (Figure 8.1).

Jill Guido, Fred Mayes and Jim Franz have all been made available to the project for a maximum of one third of their working week, 15 hours per week each. From the implementation plan there are 22 weeks of work. Multiplying these 22 weeks by the 15 hours each person is available gives a total of 330 hours. Add the extra 10 per cent for the enhancement work to reach 363 or 370 rounded up. Therefore, the

TEAM	Week Number	1	2	3	4	5	6	7	8	9	10
Name: **Guido**	Do task letter	A	B	B	E	E	E	F		H	
BD CW PG TW LL FP PL / 7 7 9 6 5 6 9	Training and meetings	tm	i	tm		tm	s		pm	c,ll	s
Review task... ...			a	b		e	e				h
Name: **Mayes**	Do task letter	A	C	C	E	E	E	G	G		
BD CW PG TW LL FP PL / 3 4 8 5 8 6 6	Training and meetings	tm	i	tm		tm	s	i		bd	s
Review task... ...			a	c		e	e		g	g	
Name: **Franz**	Do task letter	A			D	D	D	D	L		
BD CW PG TW LL FP PL / 2 3 7 0 8 0 4	Training and meetings	tm	tw	i, tm		tm	s	i			s
Review task... ...				d		d		l			
PM to review supplier for task...		d				f	h				
Project review by PM				✓			✓			✓

Figure 8.1   Implementation plan updated

hours needed to do nothing other than carry out the project tasks are 370.

This total gives the amount of *effort* needed to complete the project, a figure to be seen as the production material needed for manufacture. For bakers, this would be the amount of cake mix to make cakes. But nothing else has been included: the training of the bakers, the energy for cooking, removing the cakes from trays, packing, transporting, the sales process and any other additional overheads. The same goes for a project, the amount of production material is calculated but there is much else to be added to the budget before the total costs are known.

Add this effort or applied hours to the top line of the budget summary (Figure 8.2).

Item Number	Description	Amount	Notes
1	Task and quality hours	370hrs	(quality=10%)

Figure 8.2   Budget summary—task and quality hours

Step 2—training and development

This is where training time is calculated. Further short calculations will produce the costs of off-site training courses as well as other development activity. Add up the boxes allocated to off-site training from the implementation plan. There is a week (or 35 hours) of off-site training for each of the team giving a total of 105 hours (only the 15 hours of project time lost that week is paid for by the project, the rest has been contributed by their line department). So budget for 45 hours. Then add up the time given to self-study, coaching or working with someone else and so on. Jill Guido is being coached on Legal Liaison in week 9, an hour a day for five days giving another 5 hours. This total of 50 hours is added to the second line of the budget summary.

Step 3—meetings

Work out the cost of all planned meetings. These should be divided into two types: project team communications and customer quality communications.

Project team communications
Add up internal meetings: project team meetings, task briefings, individual meetings (but not including coaching again), team social events (if these are held outside working hours then don't include these hours in the budget but do include the actual costs of the events themselves—food, drink, transport). Remember to include travelling time to meetings if it is needed and your own time as project manager. For the brochure project a couple of hours per day or 10 hours per week should be ample.

Three team meetings of two hours each have also been planned giving a total of 24 hours for project team meetings. In addition each activity leader will need briefing as the activity start date nears. Allow 1 hour for each person involved (project manager and task member) giving 16 hours. Planned individual meetings of one hour will take another 5 hours of the project manager's time and the same for the team member being met, totalling 10 hours. Social events will be held in the middle of the project and at the end. There are no task hours for this but some money will be needed to buy the drinks and pizzas.

Customer quality communications

There are three project review meetings with the project customer for the project manager. Each meeting lasts two hours; total 6 hours. There are also 15 task reviews for the team members at one hour each. These come to a total of 21 hours. In all, step 3 needs 71 hours which are added to the third line of the Budget Summary.

Step 4—rework allowance

This is to allow for lost documentation, missed messages or other minor mishaps. It is not for the reworking of tasks, rework happens on most projects. In some organisations or in business sectors such as IT project rework can more than double the project budget. Whatever the figure is for your organisation or sector add it in percentage terms in line 4. Because you have been applying best practice all the way through your planning process a low figure can be added here. Assume an additional 2 per cent of the total tasks and quality hours (8 hours) for this brochure project.

Step 5—absenteeism and unallocated time

All organisations have absenteeism rates—this includes time when people were expected at work and were not—so illness, compassionate absence and so on is included here. Add the absentee rate in percentage for your organisation in line 5. If your organisation does not keep such information then work out a reasonable rate for yourself. An average of five days' absence in a year is about 2.12 per cent (5 absent days divided by 235 working days). For the brochure project a figure of 2 per cent or 8 hours has been used.

The best implementation plans have unallocated time or 'holes' in them. It is unlikely that each task will follow on perfectly neatly from the previous one. The brochure plan has 'holes' in weeks 8 and 9 for Jill Guido; week 7 for Fred Mayes and Jim Franz. They cannot be allocated to another project for such a short time so the 'holes' have to be paid for in the budget. Add up the holes in the implementation plan and add them to the budget summary. In this case it is 4 weeks at 15 hours, a total of 60 hours. So, including absenteeism, add 68 hours to line 5 of the budget summary (Figure 8.3).

Item Number	Description	Amount	Notes
1	Task and quality hours	370	(quality=10%)
2	Training and development hours	50	
3	Team, individual and customer meetings	71	Social events £120
4	Rework allocation	8	2% of task hours
5	Absenteeism and unallocated hours	68	2% absenteeism

Figure 8.3   Budget summary

A source of stress

The original task hours of 370 have now grown to 567 hours for the full implementation of the project to best practice standards. For many project managers, experienced and otherwise, this is a staggering realisation. Many projects are delivered with only the task hours calculated. This is the equivalent of trying to produce the brochure with a total of 370 hours planned and budgeted for; or, in percentage terms, a shortfall of 35 per cent of the 567 hours actually needed. Hence project teams can work all the hours that God gives only to fail anyway. Implementing this project in 370 hours is 'mission impossible'; it cannot be done to quality within the bounds of reasonable working hours.

It will be said that many organisations cannot afford to work to the standard of best practice outlined here. That may be true but neither can the additional 197 hours needed be ignored entirely. Meetings with the project team and briefings have to take place as well as customer face-to-face sessions. Thinking that somehow they will be 'fitted in' is sloppy planning which has foreseeable consequences for all members of the project team. This is from where the unreasonable stress on project teams often comes. Remember:

Plans which concentrate only on task hours have stress built in from the beginning.

The difference between the two figures above is the utilisation percentage; in this case 65 per cent. To deliver the project according to the plan will utilise the team for 65 per cent of the total project time. The other 35 per cent is spent doing essential work in support of project implementation but not on tasks themselves.

Before the days of privatisation of state industries, I worked with a project manager in a naval dockyard who told me quietly one day that his utilisation figure was 25 per cent. When he was planning, only 2 hours out of eight per day could be spent delivering tasks. This rate of effort was economically unsustainable in the long term but nonetheless he had to plan at the rate of 25 per cent utilisation to produce a defensible plan that bore any resemblance to reality. This example is extreme but at the other end of the spectrum project utilisation rates in excess of 90 per cent will ultimately see projects heading for trouble. A utilisation rate of 90 per cent can only mean that there is little or no leadership and all efforts are expended on task delivery with the associated risks to morale, team work and so on. Ultimately, the project will be seen as poorly run and the project manager a slave driver who doesn't deliver despite the stress.

Hours to money

Working in hours is fine but if there is a need to work in monetary values the simplest way of converting hours to money is to take the average all up hourly costs of the people who will be working on the project, multiplied by the total hours. Jill Guido, Fred Mayes and Jim Franz show an average of around £24 an hour. Multiplying 567 hours by the hourly rate of £24 gives a project labour cost circa £13 600 plus expenses and all materials.

Final Internal Budget Summary

The project needs a total of 567 hours at an estimated average of £24 per hour giving a total staff cost of	£13 600
Overtime contingency (2%)	£275
Off-site training programmes will cost 3 courses × £1000	£3 000
Bonus and penalty pot 5% (for staff bonuses and any possible penalties for late delivery to suppliers by you)	£680
Travel expenses etc	£350
Project managers allocated costs (planning etc)	£2 000
Total	£19 905

This is an accurate internal cost indicator of a project delivered to best practice. It can be delivered for less than £20 000. On top of this is added the cost of any external work—photography, distribution, printing and so on but the management of the activities are covered for in the budget.

If this total is well over any budgetary indicator given, it is important to resist the temptation to just start reducing cost. This has been planned carefully and this budget is the result of that careful planning. Reducing cost willy-nilly to come in below some arbitrary indicative figure will cancel the benefit of this careful planning. If the budget is simply unrealistic then retrace the planning in two broad steps.

First, go back to your advisors and show them your working and ask them where you could reduce costs. Something has to give way if the budgetary constraint is to be met. Either more time, better people, more risk, lower quality or less control. All these will reduce costs. Having done that, if still significantly outside guideline figures then take the second step and go back to the project definition. This project cannot be delivered according to best practice for the suggested budget. Either the project definition changes or the budget increases if project quality is to be delivered.

The budget now needs to be justified and that usually involves persuading someone to give the money and resources needed. This persuasion exercise is addressed in the next chapter.

Selling the Defensible Plan

All beginnings are delightful; the threshold is the place to pause.
Johann von Goethe (1749–1832)

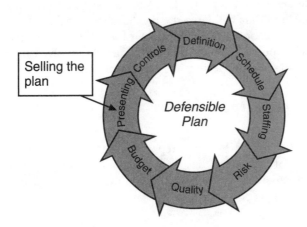

You are about to move your Defensible Plan into the public domain and it is a good time to pause at this threshold and reflect. Walk yourself slowly through the plan checking for consistency and coherence. Does it deliver what you have been asked to do; are all your assumptions and decisions defensible in the eyes of others?

When you present your plan you are engaged in a persuasion exercise and persuasion is the selling of ideas to others. A well-presented mediocre project plan is often accepted but a poorly presented workable plan frequently fails. Selling has been described as a 'conversation with a purpose' so prepare to have a conversation with a purpose with those to whom the plan needs to be sold.

Presentation options

Depending upon the culture of your organisation you might have some choices about how you present your plan. These include:

■ a conversation
■ a presentation to a boss (one-to-one)

■ a presentation to a decision-making team
■ a written submission.

Let's take them one by one.

Conversation

If possible choose this option. It is the easiest to prepare for and it is also the method that will have the best project focus. An informal, easy and open discussion with an exchange of ideas is what is needed but it is not always possible. There are fewer agenda involved in one-to-one discussions making the persuasion exercise simpler.

One-to-one presentation

This is a good option but the preparing of a presentation will increase the amount of work that has to be done. Try to bring it back to an informal discussion if at all possible. Do not offer to make a presentation if a briefing is possible.

A presentation to a decision-making team

This is the most difficult and needs the most work before the presentation is actually done. Each person on the team will have their own agenda and their personal visions of success. The HR manager will want to know what you are doing about the development of people, how much of your budget you are spending and whether it fits in with department plans. The finance manager will be looking for reduced expenditure and confirmation that the project is value for money. The user will want to know whether the project deliverable will work. And the programme manager will look at the project in a holistic way, seeking assurance that the overall project plan is deliverable. The sales manager will be looking for a final product that will support sales efforts.

It is essential that you know what dynamics are in play amongst the decision-making team before you present to them. Some of these issues can be found out whilst agreeing the agenda; make contact with each person in the decision-making team to ask them what they are looking for from your presentation.

A written submission

These are less common but in some organisations they are still the primary method of assessing project plan viability. Although written presentations can be time consuming they do have the advantage of clarity. In the process of getting a project plan down on paper clearly and concisely, woolly thinking tends to become exposed and removed. If you do have to submit a written plan ensure that there is an executive summary at the start of the document with a sentence or two only for each of the sections of the Defensible Plan. This will help get across the key points of your plan to senior managers who are unlikely to read the whole document. It is worth including the project definition in full, to ensure that there is no misunderstanding about what the project is to do. The overall structure follows the Defensible Plan but adds an introduction at the front (which includes grateful thanks to those who helped) followed by the executive summary.

Keep the language tight using short sentences and short words—they are easier to read for people in a hurry. Place anything not specifically written for the project as an appendix at the back. Remember to number the pages and add a contents page. Ask a colleague to read it to hear if the document persuades and listen carefully to the feedback. Make the changes necessary and submit.

Agenda for presentations

Do not assume that you know what the agenda will be—ask. Seeking information about the presentation agenda is an excellent way of extracting the real needs of the person or people being presented to. Offer your own outline agenda at least a week before your presentation (you don't need to complete your project plan before requesting agenda information). Write a polite memorandum thanking the decision-making team for making themselves available and then ask them for comment on the agenda. The agenda can follow the structure of the Defensible Plan built so far thus leaving out Controls for the time being. The agenda could look like this:

- Project Definition
- Schedule
- Staffing
- Risk
- Quality
- Budget
- Agreement to roll out the implementation plan.

In any event avoid presenting your budget too early, especially if you need to spend more than was at first thought necessary. Present your persuasive arguments first and then the costs of delivering your excellent plan!

No surprises

There is an old saying that says 'no surprises in the boardroom'; it is good advice. It is not a good idea to present contentious issues in your plan if you have not made those affected aware of your intentions. It is not clever to present radically new material at a presentation which has been known about for some time.

For example, in an organisation where I worked, I was joined in the boardroom by a new service director and a personal director. After a few weeks they were to be seen huddled in corners having whispered conversations. After a month of this, they asked for an hour to make a presentation to the board (I was sales director). The board duly assembled in the chairman's office and a presentation was made. As it rolled out it grew embarrassing. The main thrust was a series of cuts which would remove £1–£1.5m from expenditure—largely from marketing and sales. It was suggested that all sales staff should stop using hotels when away from home and instead were to use cheaper boarding houses. Petrol-driven company cars were to be replaced by cheaper diesels and so on. All rather obvious and rather patronising in thinking that these things had not been considered before and of course, they had. The company had a sophisticated sales force who had the difficult job of selling financial concepts in a competitive market. They were well selected and trained and had choices about whether or not they would choose to live in boarding houses and drive diesel cars and so on. Losing our best people to voracious competitors as well as hitting the recruitment effort in a growing market was probably not a good idea. At the end the chairman, a kindly man, thanked the two directors and suggested that if they could get only four additional members of the sales force on target, then those savings would be covered by their sales alone.

Our new colleagues had succeeded in embarrassing themselves and their departments whilst at the same time injuring relationships through thinly-veiled attacks on management of parts of the business about which they knew little. Finding out the lie of the land would have served them so much better. If they had taken the trouble to talk openly with any one other of the board members, they would have found out the policies of the chairman and chief executive. Surprising senior managers is a risky venture and should not be attempted in project presentations. Rather, be open and try to persuade any potential dissent before the presentation meeting.

Confirming the agenda

Having found out what people want to hear, write a draft agenda and circulate it to the people coming asking for comments by a specific time.

The presentation

As a guide, take no more than twenty minutes for your presentation—managers get bored of being presented to. Allow at least a further fifteen minutes for questions. Keep the presentation material at a high level and don't present detail—have the detail prepared and take it with you in case of questions, but keep it out of the main presentation. Be clear about what is wanted from the decision-making team and include it in the presentation objectives (see 'getting agreement' below).

Don't tell them what they already know other than as a brief reminder—you don't have time. Concentrate on assumptions made and how the whole plan fits together in delivering the project. In planning the presentation use work breakdown structure, adding timings at the bottom of each column (Figure 9.1). In this way you will prepare only what there is time for rather than preparing more than can be delivered, resulting in talking too quickly and confusingly in an attempt to present it all.

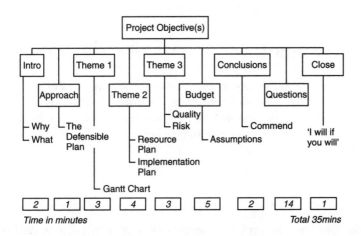

Please respond with any comments to Gordon Webster on ext 3476 by Wednesday 23rd November

Figure 9.1   Project presentation—proposed structure, content and timing

Once you have the responses to the agenda you can circulate your work breakdown structure for approval. If a team member fails to understand they can always ring for clarification before the presentation. Ensure you put your telephone contact number on the plan.

Notice the timings underneath the boxes so that people know what to expect. They will also see the degree of emphasis on various topics. As said earlier Controls are not yet included. Until the plan is approved the information needed for building accurate Controls is not yet available. Budget allocations may be changed or the number of people available to deliver the project may be changed so the base data needed to draw up controls is not yet 'fixed'. However, for your presentation ensure that you know what your key Control measures will be, even though you cannot yet finalise them.

Question handling

Leave plenty of time for questions. Get agreement at the start that only questions of clarity will be accepted during the presentation or else you could lose control of the presentation. Questions about content or the challenging of assumptions should come at the end. During questions be careful not to lose time by allowing domination by one person or one subject, beware of too many supplementary questions coming from persons with an axe to grind. Allow one or two supplementary questions and then say that you'll come back if there is time and then take questions from others. The project owner or sponsor goes first unless there is a more senior person in the room to whom deference is due.

Get agreement

The whole purpose of your presentation is to win agreement for the plan. Ensure that you ask for permission to proceed within the parameters presented. If you are drawn into negotiation, do not become reckless and give away your carefully planned resources, this is a Defensible Plan so defend it.

Power

A common problem at group presentations and in particular during questioning centres around power. Presenting with assertion can challenge the power and esteem of managers. If the presentation is over-assertive then a power-sensitive manager can challenge a method or reduce a resource needed just to let everybody know who is boss. It is best not to get into this territory. If you are being pressed hard to accept a decision that is worrisome, then buy time and ask to look at the issue again and make an appointment to discuss it with the manager concerned. This subsequent meeting is more likely to be one-to-one with fewer undercurrents of power. Don't get into a stand-off unless it is fundamental to the plan—the chances are you won't win and you will have got your project off to a bad start. Work with managers and not against them—you need them on your side.

Written summary

Prepare the written summary last of all. Too many project managers spend hours writing up project plans for presentation and then leave too little time for their verbal presentation. Do the verbal presentation first and then produce a short tight summary (including any visuals). Most managers do not have time to read reports. They will flick to the summary and budget and make decisions from there. All the above depends on what happens in your organisations. If a written submission before verbal presentation is the norm, keep the verbal presentation to the salient points of the plan, leaving more time for questions. The written submission should end with a document asking for permission to proceed.

Confirmation

Assuming that you succeed in the persuasion exercise write and thank the people who came. Answer any questions or take the opportunity to answer again any questions that you felt could have been dealt with better during the presentation itself and then assure them of your best endeavours.

Having succeeded and agreed final figures, set up your project controls (as shown in Chapter 11). But before doing that read the overview of project implementation that follows in the next chapter which explains why Controls are more than just measures of quantity.

Part II
Implementing the Defensible Plan

Project implementation, an overview

This new attitude towards effort and work as an aim in itself, may be assumed the most important psychological change which has happened to man since the Middle Ages. The development of a frantic activity and a striving to do something . . .
Erich Fromm *Psychoanalytical Theorist*

Your plan has been accepted. Take a congratulatory break to draw breath before turning your thoughts to implementation. For many people, project implementation can conjure up protracted periods of frantic activity. At best it is a time of excitement and challenge, promoting a 'can-do' attitude amongst those involved; provided the activity results from the implementation of a well-prepared plan. If, however, this frantic activity is taking place in an effort just to keep pace or to catch up, then the project team members will feel less positive about repeated demands for yet more frenetic haste. Be sure that any activity during the implementation phase is under proper control.

Project implementation is primarily about people. Only people can produce work and effort so your first concern must be how to lead and motivate your team. To help understand implementation more fully revisit the John Adair leadership model in Chapter 5. It was used to help build an effective leadership plan. It can be applied equally effectively for the project implementation phase. Let us remind ourselves what was said:

The project manager needs to address three principal areas; the achievement of the task, the satisfaction of individual needs and the maintenance of the team. The successful delivery of the task or the project can only be achieved using individuals who are motivated through the satisfaction of their own needs, preferably working in a cohesive team which is being maintained by the actions (leadership) of the project manager. These three activities are represented as three spheres of equal size (Figure 10.1). It is the job of the project leader to keep these spheres in balance. If they become out of balance then the project becomes more difficult to lead.

Taking each of the spheres in turn you will see that during your planning phase all of them were covered. A work breakdown structure of the implementation plan built in previous chapters displays (Figure 10.2) much of what is needed to implement the project successfully. The Task column has rather more activities in it than the other two and this is not untypical. However, the Individual Needs and Team Maintenance

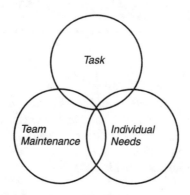

Figure 10.1   The three spheres

columns provide other leadership elements such as individual motivation and team building, which spin out of these planned activities.

A common problem during project implementation is the abandon-
ment of all leadership activities when the task falls behind. Meetings are
cancelled and people are put under pressure to work harder and more
unreasonably. This typical response to a late schedule is an over concentration on the task circle, when it is more likely that the individual and
team circles need attention. The task circle may already be too big
where people are being asked to focus only on task thereby taking away
inputs from the other two circles. This absence of leadership can make
existing troubles worse. There are many reasons why this is done. Our
thinking preferences can help us understand why this behaviour occurs

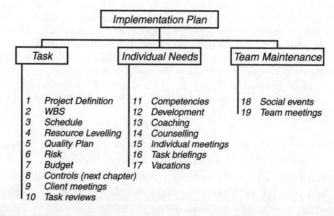

Figure 10.2   Work breakdown of an implementation plan

during project implementation; where it comes from and how it impacts decisions made.

We have all met people who, although bright and capable in a given area or skill, seem totally incapable at something apparently much more simple. The 'absent minded professor' is an extreme example. Quantum theory is no problem for them but the household accounts are beyond their understanding. A more businesslike example might be the business strategist who has the vision to see what shape the business has to be for the future but cannot see how to get there. In both these examples the people observed have strong dominances in how they choose to think.

Ned Herrmann, in his book *The Creative Brain* (Brain Books, 5th edn, 1994), has been most helpful in metaphorically mapping out four thinking style dominances open to us as project managers. He takes the basic concept of left and right brain thinking and expands it out into four quadrants. Left brain thinking is described as logical, analytical, step-by-step and structured. Right brain thinking is considered more emotional, imaginative, creative and unstructured. Herrmann has added the upper and lower hemispheres. The upper sphere is about a cerebral approach, intellectual intuition and 'head' thinking. The lower is largely about emotional intuition, or 'gut' instinct—those fight or flight, feeding and reproduction instincts from prehistoric times (Figure 10.3).

At some time or another we will use all four thinking styles, but most of us use one or two more frequently. Our choice is a mix of genetics and experience but we tend to use constantly those thinking styles that have been successful for us in the past. There are also external influences which will influence which of the styles is used. For example, if

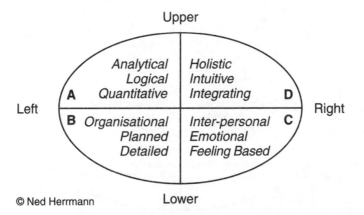

Figure 10.3   Herrmann thinking styles: four quadrants, labelled anticlockwise A–D

you go back to your years in school, college or university in which quadrant were you predominantly taught? Unless you specialised in, for example, the performing arts, your education was likely to have been delivered on the left side of the metaphor. Highly-structured learning with repeated requests to 'explain your logic' or 'show your working' even though you knew the right answer. Later on, working within an organisation, it is likely that your thinking, too, is measured on the left, through financial performance. And to that can be added the ever-growing use of the most left-brained piece of equipment of all—the computer. These combined influences push us further over to the left and away from the right—more than is good for project implementation.

Over the past eight years I have been using the Herrmann model with project managers. I begin by asking them to make lists about what it is that project managers do. I then ask them to plot these activities over the Herrmann model. This produces feedback (Figure 10.4) to be incorporated into the assignment I then set them.

All the quadrants have many activities; it can be seen that to be effective, project managers must use the thinking of all the quadrants. Therefore, the effective project leader is required to operate in all quadrants at some time or another during project delivery.

For most of us, operating in all quadrants is not easy; it is unlikely that you will be able to use the thinking styles equally competently. From Herrmann's research we know that less than 5 per cent of the population are able to do this.

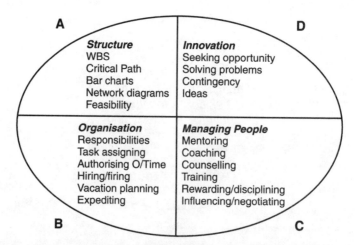

Figure 10.4 Project management activity applying Herrmann's metaphor

There is also tension across the diagonals of the model. If A quadrant is used with its logical thinking you want to know the *facts* and as a result you may not consider the people aspects of the C quadrant well enough.

The C quadrant wants motivated people who are listened to and who work in teams to deliver the project. *Feelings* and motivation are most important and too many facts get in the way of operating from this emotional base.

The B quadrant wants things done to a procedure, using the right resources at the right time in the right place as per the plan. Success is a result of efficiency and structure. All activities are to *conform* with the plan and flexibility is not needed when the plan is finished, change is not a strong point.

Yet for the D quadrant the importance of being able to imagine and fantasise is all important. Fertile creativity can take leaps into the *future* in a way that leaves colleagues breathless. Structure or what already exists is unlikely to be considered, these matters simply get in the way of this totally flexible thinking style.

So whilst using only your own preferred styles you will omit or not give enough importance to activities from other less attractive quadrants. Accepting that all the activities above are essential to a well executed project implementation, then learning to use your less preferred quadrants is a must. This learning experience can feel like writing with the other hand. Initially it does not feel right but with practice it can be done quite quickly.

In the course of running development programmes for project managers I have been able to apply an instrument developed by Herrmann which determines the quadrant preferences of people in the room. The results allow project managers as individuals, as well as groups, to know their own preferences. Invariably a group profile shows a left brain preference. It would appear that managers in groups prefer to be logical and analytical in their thinking styles.

To understand the impact of this left brain preference, you can add the results of this exercise to Herrmann's model (Figure 10.5).

The left hemisphere has gained the word *Task*. The right hemisphere has gained the word *Process*. They are almost in conflict with each other. The left uses facts, structure and procedures to get things done, while the right wants to know about the opportunities that exist and has concern for the motivation and leadership of people. When under pressure you move to your dominant quadrant, which for project managers in general means a move towards task activity. It is done at the expense of right hemisphere activities. That is why project managers under pressure will focus all efforts on task delivery when in fact it may be better to reduce task effort. It is asking managers to go slower so that they might go faster! It screams against logic.

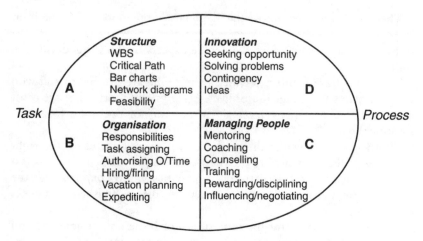

Figure 10.5   Additions to Herrmann

Leadership and motivation—which live in the right hemisphere—are acts of faith. Coaching, counselling, motivation, leadership are all 'touchy feely' words and activities that lack the immediacy of direct action. Faith is not a strong point of left-brained groups. A typical comment heard is 'The time spent taking my guys out for a beer and a pizza would be better spent progressing the project, and anyway my boss never takes me for a beer!'

Yet it is motivated people operating in teams that best deliver projects. If the right hemisphere activities of meetings, training and so on are switched off immediately the pressure comes on then it follows that people will cease to be motivated or developed. Team behaviour will decline and ultimately the project could fail. Project managers do this all the time meaning that most of them consciously struggle to hold a leadership line.

During the building of the Defensible Plan and in particular the leadership elements in Chapter 5, it may be felt that the process was moving away from the building of a plan. To balance a strong pull to the left hemisphere you must focus hard on what your people need, as individuals and as teams, early in the process. It therefore should be done during the building of the Defensible Plan. Left to our own devices and desires it is not what most of us would choose to do.

Herrmann gives a metaphorical view of best practice project leadership. The dangers of over emphasis on logic, analysis, administration and structure can be seen; and so too the dangers of left brain only approaches to project implementation. People (and customers) need to be led from the right brain where their emotions can be engaged and motivated to your chosen route.

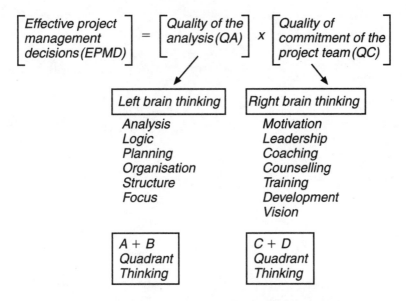

Figure 10.6   Effective decisions are 'whole brained'

To summarise this overview of project implementation it can be said that the project manager needs to be in the business of making effective decisions—constantly. These decisions will be implemented effectively more often if all the thinking style quadrants are employed. Use the logic, structure, planning and analysis of the left hemisphere together with the flexibility and consideration for the involvement and motivation of people from the right hemisphere.

From that all the elements of the chapter can be pulled together using the formula EPMD = QA × QC (Figure 10.6).

Effective decisions on projects are a product of a balance between capable analysis of the situation and the commitment of the people on the team. The overall message is to avoid focusing entirely on the task. The task is delivered by people who need to be led using right brain thinking. The controls that are to be set up to help implement projects use mostly left-brain measurement. However, the indicators on these controls are moved by the actions of people; it is therefore people that you must lead to move those indicators to the desired place—and not the other way round.

Building and using project controls

A trend is a trend is a trend,
But the question is, will it bend?
Will it alter its course,
Through some unforeseen force
And come to a premature end?
Alec Cairncross *Economics Journal* (1969)

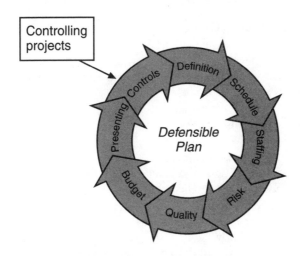

Trends help to forecast the future. If contributory factors remain constant then the existing trend will continue. But trends will only remain
the same if forces seen and unseen do not come into play—in projects
they always do in one way or another. You therefore need a set of controls to see trends from which to attempt with a degree of accuracy to
forecast the future. Although your Defensible Plan has been presented
this is its final part. Controls cannot be built until after final agreement
on schedules and budgets. If they are built before final agreement, any
changes will mean that they have to be done again.

'Control' is a powerful word. It influences our social, cultural and
economic structures. Control can be seen in two ways: first, in a very
positive light as it allows the measurement of success. For example, a
winning Olympian is grateful for the quality controls that permit the

declaration of a new record. When exceeding sales targets or meeting deadlines it is a positive reflection of the controls that allow us to make these claims. Secondly, control can be seen as a tool to beat subordinates over a supposed lack of results. Unfortunately, many people will have experienced this view.

In such negative circumstances staff avoid using measures to report performance. Project controls need to be of the first, positive, variety.

This chapter is in two parts: the first explains the components of a good project control system and the second advises on where to get the necessary information and how best to use it.

Part one—the components of a good control system

To understand what a good control system does for a project manager, observe a pilot of a small aircraft. Making her way over the countryside, she needs to know:

- at what height she is flying;
- her direction;
- how much fuel she is burning;
- that she is flying straight and level;
- her air speed;
- her engine revolutions.

She also needs to know where she is, what the wind is doing, the weather forecast, local radio frequencies and so on. All this she will resolve before she leaves the ground when filing her flight plan.

In flight, she will check these crucial items of information by referring to her instrument panel (Figure 11.1).

The pilot's instruments show her that she is flying at 5000 feet at 180 knots in a northerly direction. She is burning fuel at a rate of 90 units per hour. The Climb/Descent indicator tells whether she is going up or down. The 'Attitude' dial indicates the position of her aircraft relative to the horizon and whether it is flying straight and level—important when flying into cloud and the ground can't be seen.

Continuing on the journey for a further 15 minutes, the pilot will note changes in the cockpit instruments (Figure 11.2). She is now flying at 5500 feet and her speed has dropped to 140 knots whilst burning fuel at the rate of 100. She is still heading north but is climbing and the aircraft's nose is above the horizon. She now asks herself, 'What has happened in the cockpit to produce such a change? What did I do?'

Simple Flight Control System

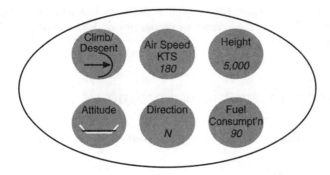

Figure 11.1   Instrument panel. A Few details have been added to each dial

The answer is that she pulled back gently on the stick and slowly started to climb. The information available allowed her to deduct what had happened in the cockpit.

Interlocking and overlapping

The pilot (project manager) in one simple action—pulling back on the stick—made several of the dials (project controls) move. Good controls are therefore overlapping and interlocking and help you identify what actions produced which reactions in your projects. Information which exists in isolation, standing alone, is of much less use. Climbing into a

Simple Flight Control System

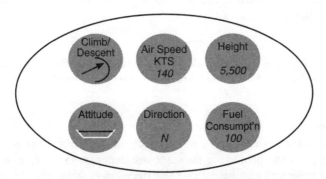

Figure 11.2   Changes observed

larger aircraft you will see a lot more dials, but many of them are in support of the main indicators—the main controls. These main controls will move first, alerting the pilot if something has changed. The pilot will then move onto the myriad of secondary dials that help find exactly what has changed.

Historical, diagnostic and prognostic

Good information as opposed to data comes in three different ways:

1 Past (historical).
2 Present (diagnostic).
3 Future (prognostic).

The past is of interest because it got you to where you are now. The present indicates current performance against plan and from the two it can be seen what is likely to happen if you continue in this way. The future is what interests the project manager because he or she can impact it. For example, the pilot climbed the aircraft 1000 feet in 15 minutes. If she left things the same, in half an hour she would have been 2000 feet higher.

The past cannot be changed, the present can be understood but only the future can be changed. Project managers particularly want to know about the future. Good controls will tell you what you need to do to ensure that the future moves in the desired direction.

Features of a good control system

A good control system needs a number of positive features. Some are discussed here.

Visible
On the wall of the office for all to see, regardless of the progress. Most are on the wall when things are going well and in the bottom desk drawer when they are not.

Accurate
The information used to plot the controls must reflect what is actually happening on the project. If they are not accurate they are a waste of valuable time and can be a basis for decision-making about problems that don't exist, whilst being misleading about problems that do exist.

Reliable
They should report the same information in the same way throughout the project.

Valid
Do the figures measure what they are supposed to be reporting? Does an absence of customer complaints mean that customers are delighted? Does an absence of formal complaints from the project team mean that morale is high? In both cases the answer can only be maybe. Better measurement is needed for accurate reporting.

Timely
The information needs to be timely and up to date. There is little point in having vital information a week after it is needed for decision-making.

Prognostic
The control system should give the project manager a view of the future. 'If the project continues in this way, this will happen.'

Brochure project—the control panel

The controls needed to produce the brochure project follow the above principles: a set of controls along with information about how they are built. All that is needed to 'fly' a project is these controls together with your:

- implementation plan
- logic network
- budget
- bar chart.

Control chart number 1—performance

This control tells how much effort has been put into the project against how much was planned. The performance control measures how well the project leader is managing the resources of the project but it is more than just a measure of effort in and product out. The drivers of performance are motivation, communication, confidence, appropriate leadership and an accurate fit between the needs of project team members and the job they are given to do; are they round pegs in round holes? It also reflects the existence or otherwise of teamwork and team leadership by the project manager. A well performing project team is

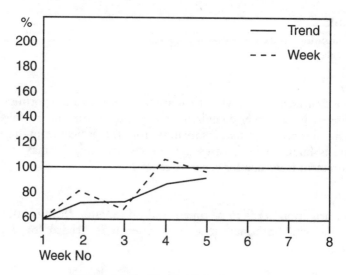

Figure 11.3   Project performance

difficult to grow and this control will help in gauging whether the project manager is succeeding or not. More will be said about the interpretation of this control later in the chapter.

To build the chart (Figure 11.3) use a range of 60–200 per cent for the vertical axis and draw a horizontal line representing a baseline of 100 per cent performance. At the end of each week you will be able to calculate the performance of your project for that week and for the project to date, hence the two lines. The weekly line will oscillate but the project to date trend line is the most valuable indicator telling you whether performance is going steadily up or down.

The weekly performance is reported using a dotted line and the solid line is the project to date (which is the total of all the project implementation weeks so far averaged). On the week-by-week basis this project performance is rather up and down, however the project trend is steadily upwards.

Control chart number 2—staff utilisation

Utilisation is the percentage of the total project hours that are being used directly on tasks and quality only, against the plan. For the brochure, utilisation hours represent 65 per cent of the total project hours so this is the base line. If utilisation hours go over the base line then they are being taken away from elsewhere. If it is from a reduction

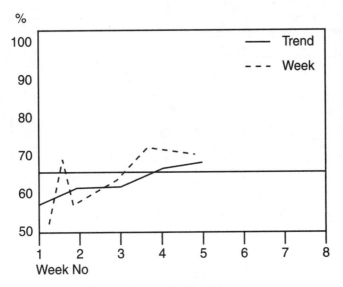

Figure 11.4   Staff utilisation

of activity in other areas, the impact of this will need to be known. If the hours are higher because people are putting in more hours voluntarily, then ensure that they don't do this for too long or the goodwill of the team will be lost. High utilisation is not sustainable for long periods as exhaustion and outside pressures intervene. For example, line managers start to complain about their people spending too much time on the project. The project is then impacted in other ways, quality suffers, morale drops and quality reduces with its associated rework and added costs and delays.

To build the utilisation chart (Figure 11.4), use a range of 50–100 per cent on the vertical axis and draw a horizontal line representing planned staff utilisation. For the brochure, the task and quality hours are 65 per cent of the total hours for the project so this becomes the utilisation base line.

Again, two lines are used to report status—one for the week and one for the project to date. Here the weekly utilisation varies but the project to date trend line is steadily rising. At week 5 it is climbing above the base line so the project manager needs to know why this is happening so that action can be taken if it continues to climb.

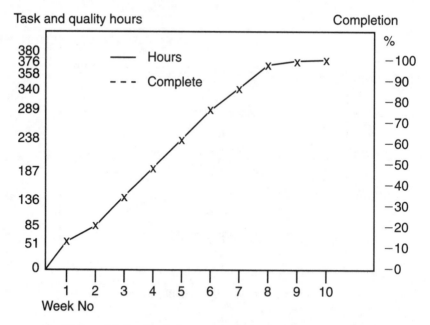

Figure 11.5   Task hours and percentage complete

Control chart number 3—task hours and completion

This control chart shows the relationship between the task and quality hours spent on the project and the progress made. The chart (Figure 11.5) has two vertical axes: one for the hours that were spent actually doing tasks and enhancements; and another for the percentage complete of the project. The shared, identical base line is taken from the budget. For the brochure, there are 370 task and enhancement hours and a further 8 hours for rework; round up this total to 380. The base line in this case will not be straight, implementation hours are not constant as people leave and join the project from week to week.

For each week of the plan take the number of people working on the project, multiply by 15 to get their task hours and then add 10 per cent for the quality hours. Round up the numbers as there is no need for decimals. The running weekly total will give the base line.

To get the corresponding completion figure for the other vertical axis, calculate the percentage complete the project should be for the planned hours spent. Utilise again the implementation plan, adding the requisite data (Figure 11.6). For example the brochure in week 1 plans to use 51

Week No	1	2	3	4	5	6	7	8	9	10
Weekly Task Hours	45	30	45	45	45	45	45	15	15	0
+10% Quality + 1 hour for rework	6	4	6	6	6	6	6	3	3	0
Total Weekly Hours	51	34	51	51	51	51	51	18	18	0
Cumulative Weekly Hours (Left hand scale)	51	85	136	187	238	289	340	358	376	380
% Complete (Right hand scale)	13	22	36	49	63	76	89	94	99	100

Figure 11.6   Task hours and completion table

hours. Divide this 51 by the total task project hours of 380 to get a completion figure of 13 per cent for the end of that week. Week 2 has a total of 85 hours which means that the project should be 22 per cent complete according to plan. Continue up the weeks adding the percentage complete to the right hand scale.

Using the above numbers the control chart can be drawn using the two bottom rows as scales. Task hours on the left and completion on the right. They share a common base line but it is easier to draw using the percentage complete scale. Having done that enter the hours corresponding to the percentage complete on the left scale.

Control chart number 4—forecast final hours

This control is used to trend the expenditure of effort. During the opening weeks of the project the forecast final hours (Figure 11.7) will appear very high. This is because although started, very little is being completed as people settle in and time is spent briefing and training. However, it should then track steadily downwards to the end of the project. If the trend line plummets or starts to rise violently then there is a variation that needs explaining and action should be taken.

Use a range of 100 to 1000 hours on the vertical axis. Draw a horizontal line representing forecast final hours of the project as agreed in the budget presentation. In the brochure example it was 567 hours, this becomes the base line (Figure 11.8).

In the early weeks of the project this chart may seem a little disconnected from the other controls. But as the project moves into busier phases it can serve as a valuable early warning of difficulty in other areas of the project. If the project is not spending what it should then there has to be a reason for it—does the project manager know?

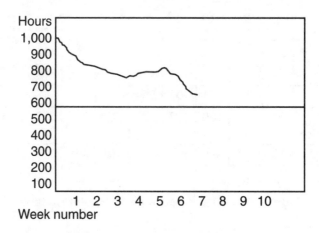

Figure 11.7   Forecast final hours

Control chart number 5—customer satisfaction

Customer satisfaction is a measurement of perceptions of quality by the customer. The most effective way of measuring it is by asking the customer at intervals how satisfied they are. The best time to do this is at review meetings. This verbal reporting is useful and it can also measure the underlying activity that should be generating satisfaction. Customer review meetings are opportunities to draw out enhancements or improvements which will delight customers.

For the brochure 10 per cent was added to budgeted hours to allow for this so there are 40 hours available. Tracking these hours will tell if the reviews and therefore the enhancement work is being done. An underspend may reflect negative comments at meetings and an overspend may indicate that additional work is no longer of the enhancement category and should be charged for. A combination of adverse comment with overspend might indicate that the skills needed are not in place and too many mistakes are being made which are observed by the customer—with a corresponding increase in enhancements. Or the psychological contract (see Chapter 7) may have been upset.

$$\frac{Hours\ spent\ to\ date}{Project\ week\ number} \times Total\ planned\ project\ weeks = Forecast\ final\ hours$$

Figure 11.8   Base line forecast hours

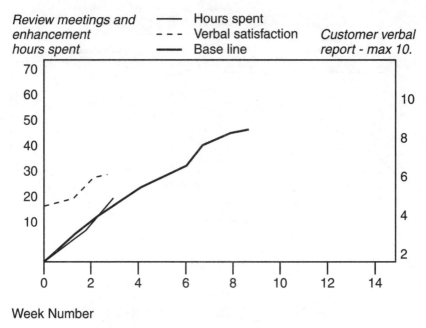

Figure 11.9   Customer satisfaction

Again, draw a graph with two scales (Figure 11.9). The right hand scale will be a mark out of 10 awarded either by the customer or assessed objectively by the project manager. The left hand scale is the total hours spent on quality. The base line is drawn from the planned cumulative hours allowed for quality and rework. For the brochure this is 46 hours. (Note that the weeks continue beyond the end of the project to week 16 ensuring quality feedback after the project has finished.)

In this example the actual hours spent is broadly tracking the base line. The verbal satisfaction is trending up as it should if the quality hours are being spent effectively.

Complete control panel or 'cockpit chart'

These controls, together with a bar chart, the network diagram, the budget and an implementation plan make a 'project flight control panel' ready for project implementation, and are shown on page 136 all together as a cockpit chart.

The Project Manager's 'Cockpit Chart'

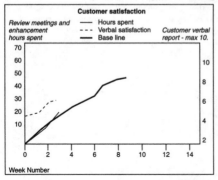

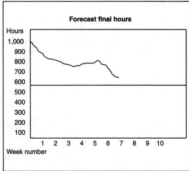

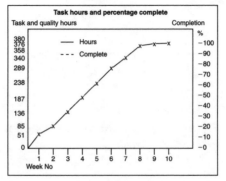

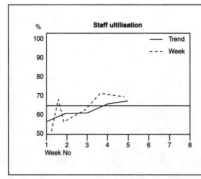

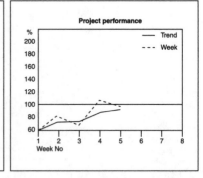

Part two—using controls to help manage our projects

Having built controls or 'cockpit charts' how do we get the information needed to build and update control charts and how are they used to read project status? The concept of 'earned value' is used, the knowledge of which is a must for any project manager. Despite its off-putting

Activity label	Actual hours spent on activity	Total hours planned for activity (inc 10% quality)	% complete at this date	*Earned value*
A	60	50	100%	50
B	35	33	66%	22
C	33	33	100%	33
D	16	66	10%	7
Totals	144			112

Figure 11.10   Project status table

title earned value is a reasonably friendly and common sense tool that is useful in knowing where you *really* are in your project.

For illustration let's take the end of week 3 of the brochure project and complete the charts. The first step is to gather what is known to build an easy reference table.

Step one—build a project status table

This table tells us what is known from a team meeting which took place this week (Figure 11.10).

All the columns are self-explanatory except for the last. Earned value is calculated by multiplying the hours planned by the completion status. For example, task B has a total of 33 hours planned and is 66 per cent complete; 66 per cent of 33 is 22 and that is the earned value.

In total, 144 hours has been spent completing work but the project has *earned* only 112 hours. The plan or 'contract' is to be paid 112 hours for the work actually completed and that is what is 'paid'. Just because more has been spent doesn't mean that you can 'pay' more. A total of only 112 hours of work has been earned according to the plan despite 144 hours having been spent.

This is the information used to complete the control charts.

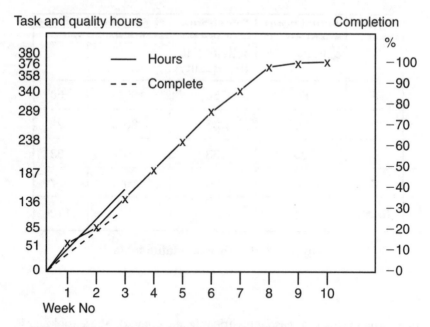

Figure 11.11   Task hours and percentage complete (week 3)

Step two—complete the task hours and completion chart

The following simple calculation is used to work out completion.

Earned Value ÷ Total Planned Task Hours = Completion

Therefore 112 ÷ 380 = 29 per cent complete.

Add the 29 per cent complete figure to the task hours and percentage complete chart (Figure 11.11) using the right hand column. Use the left hand column to enter the actual hours spent—144. Before reading this chart complete the other controls.

Step three—calculate performance

Performance is the comparison between what is put in and 'what was got out'. In week 3, 144 hours were put in but only 112 were taken out (earned value). Therefore:

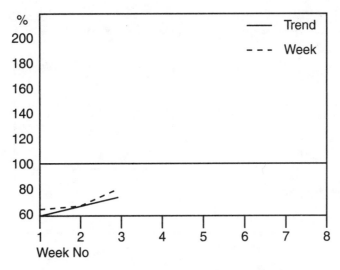

Figure 11.12   Project performance (week 3)

Earned value/total task hours spent = performance %

So: 112 ÷ 144 = a performance figure of 78 per cent. Plot this figure on the performance control chart (Figure 11.12).

Step four—calculate staff utilisation

We know that 144 hours were spent on tasks and quality. From the implementation plan it is known that the planned task hours to the end of week 3 was 136. This is the 65 per cent staff utilisation figure that was planned for in the budget; 8 hours more than planned was spent on tasks, which means that an extra 4 per cent was used—giving us a utilisation figure of 69 per cent for the end of week 3. (136 hours = 65 per cent utilisation so each 1 per cent = 2.1 hours. Therefore 8 hours = 4 per cent.) Plot this on the staff utilisation chart (Figure 11.13).

Step five—forecast final cost

Up to the end of week 3, 144 hours were spent on tasks and enhancements. There were 2 meetings of 2 hours each totalling 16 staff hours and a further 3 individual meetings of an hour totalling 6 hours. There

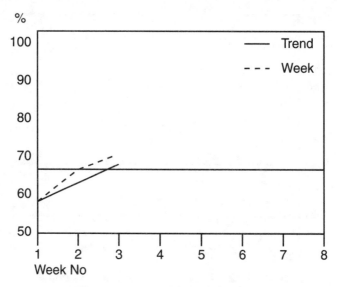

Figure 11.13   Staff utilisation

was a week of unallocated time for Franz in week 2, which means paying for his 15 hours that week as unallocated hours. There was no absenteeism. This makes a total of 181 hours. To get the final forecast hours for the week divide the 181 by the number of weeks run on the project and then multiply by the total number of project weeks planned:

$$181 \div 3 \times 10 = 603 \text{ hours}$$

Plot this on the control chart (Figure 11.14).

Step six—customer satisfaction

For the first three weeks 13 quality hours were allowed for not including rework. The three task reviews planned were held taking up a total of 4 staff hours. These meetings produced 5 enhancement requests each taking an average of 2 hours to complete. This brought a total of 14 quality hours. The customer reports a satisfaction level of 7 for the week. A file was misplaced which meant 4 hours lost to rework. Add all this to the control chart (Figure 11.15).

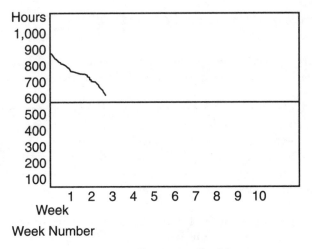

Figure 11.14   Forecast final hours

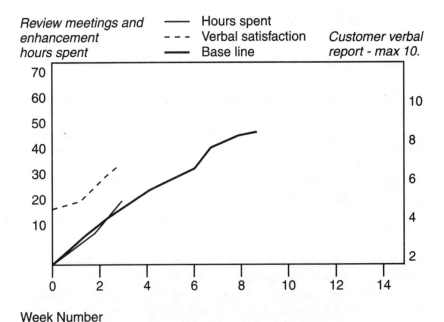

Figure 11.15   Customer satisfaction (week 3)

Control charts and early warning

The control charts are read together to draw some conclusions or define some questions that need to be answered. The project is:

■ Behind completion: 29 per cent actual against 36 per cent planned.
■ Overspent in hours: 144 hours spent against 136 planned.
■ Low in performance: 78 per cent against 100 per cent.
■ Your utilisation is trending up: above the 65 per cent (69 per cent).
■ Steadily improving in customer satisfaction: care needed to be taken over quality hours spent.

The project is not on track but it is not a disaster. Project controls illustrate quickly and simply where the project is at any given time. However, the answers to problems are not in the control panel but it does help us to ask the right questions.

This project needs to be brought back on track and it is the job of the project manager to do so. Asking the project team where they think they will be in two weeks' time at the end of week 5, produced the following response:

Activity:

A—100 per cent complete
B—100 per cent complete
C—100 per cent complete
D—80 per cent complete
E—60 per cent complete

What does this mean for the project? Using earned value, plot the prognostics of this offered situation for week 5 (Figure 11.16).

Earned value is 205 hours so percentage complete is $205 \div 380 = 54$ per cent. But is it satisfactory? Transfer it to the task hours and percentage complete chart (Figure 11.17) and see. The answer is no. Completion remains behind and although fewer hours are being used more needs to be done to get project completion fully on track. Without knowing anything other than completion and planned hours, a prognosis of an offered situation is produced.

Earned value is being used to help with a 'what if' process. There is little point in discussing the merits of a route of action if the answer it produces cannot be seen. So what will happen if we complete activities D and E by the end of week 5—what would that do for the project? Estimate what the actual task hours are using the information from previous weeks. Then complete the earned value table (Figure 11.18).

So now at the end of week 6 the project will be $250 \div 380 = 66$ per

Activity label	Actual hours spent on activity	Total hours planned for activity	% complete at this date	*Earned value*
A	60	50	100%	50
B	50	33	100%	33
C	33	33	100%	33
D	38	44	80%	35
E	60	90	60%	54
Totals	241			205

Figure 11.16   Status forecast for end of week 5

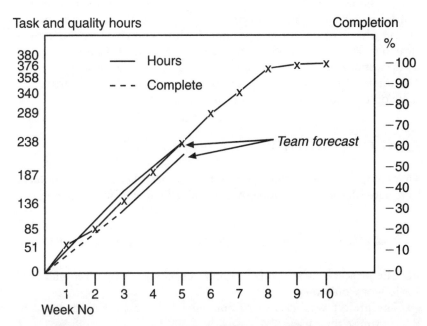

Figure 11.17   Task hours and percentage complete (forecast week 5)

Activity label	Actual hours spent on activity	Total hours planned for activity	% complete at this date	*Earned value*
A	60	50	100%	50
B	50	33	100%	33
C	33	33	100%	33
D	47	44	100%	44
E	90	90	100%	90
Totals	280			250

Figure 11.18   What if?—status forecast for end of week 5

cent complete having spent 280 task hours to get there. Plot it on the control chart (Figure 11.19).

This shows that the project completion is ahead of track provided D and E are 100 per cent complete. What needs to be done to bring the project ahead of its current position is now known. The situation is clear but whether it can be done needs to be decided. Can overtime be used or more people, consultants, etc., or is there a need to re-plan? This may mean more hours, less performance but at least there are some options about what has to be done.

End of planning

That completes the planning phase of the project. Let us take a moment to review what has been done. A Defensible Plan was built which meant that:

1 The project was *defined* for all involved to understand fully what was required.
2 The project was *scheduled* to find out what was involved and how long it would take.
3 The project was *levelled* to minimise the resources needed and to maximise their use.
4 *Leadership* was planned for ensuring that the motivation and development of project team members was considered and planned for.

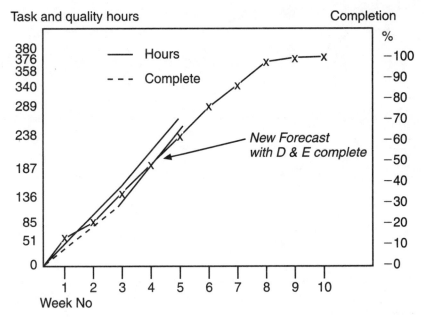

Figure 11.19   Task hours and percentage complete (What if?—
forecast week 5)

5 An *implementation plan* was developed to be used as a route map through the project delivery.
6 Problems were anticipated and planned for by producing a *risk* plan.
7 A *quality* plan was built to delight customers.
8 The whole project was costed in the *budget*.
9 A discussion or presentation was prepared to sell the Defensible Plan to gain *agreement*.
10 Having gained agreement *controls* were prepared ready for project implementation.

All this has been in preparation for the delivery of the project. It takes a considerable investment of time and mental energy, the rewards come now when you are about to roll out your plan. You are confident, you know what you are supposed to be doing and when and you will be knowledgeable with your people whether they work full-time for you or not. Stress will be much less because you have built into your plan the time you need to do things well and under control.

In the remaining chapters of the book implementation of the project will be addressed. You will be given better understanding of what is needed to ensure your carefully built project is delivered under control and with motivated people.

Leading and motivating project team members

'She still seems to me in her own way a person born to command,' said Luce. 'I wonder if anyone is born to obey,' said Isobel. 'That may be why people command rather badly, that they have no suitable material to work on!'
Ivy Compton-Burnett *Parents and Children* (1941)

Having understood in overview the issues concerning the implementation of projects let's be more specific about what needs to be considered. Chapter 5 addressed the subject of planning for the leadership of people. It is your leadership and motivation that will determine whether in the eyes of your people the project was well delivered or otherwise. And you work on the assumption that your people are 'suitable material' for leadership.

Adair advised that to deliver projects you must lead your people both as individuals and as teams. This chapter looks in more detail at the leadership of people as individuals. You will firstly understand what power bases you have available to you as project manager and how you should use them. Then you will look at leadership styles and how you should use them.

Project managers are leaders and leaders exercise power over others with the objective of getting others to do willingly what they want them to do. In the pursuit of that objective you have seven different powers which can be used either singly or in a mix of two or more. They are:

1 Coercion: use of fear and threat.
2 Legitimate: the use of formal power given to you with title of project manager, your 'rank' in the organisation.
3 Referent: the use of power of personality; an example would be use of charisma.
4 Reward: the power to give and take away.
5 Information: being 'in the know'.
6 Connection: who you know; for example the boss's secretary.
7 Expert: respected knowledge and experience in using it.

Each of these power bases are exercised using different methods of influence (Figure 12.1). For example, reward power is used to exchange what you want for what you have to give; using coercion usually implies some sort of threat—do it or else! Figure 12.1 shows the power

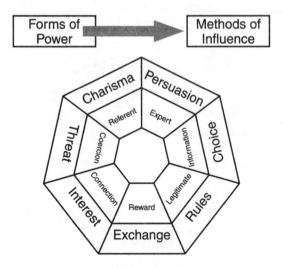

Figure 12.1   Power and influence

on the inside septagon with what that power gives the user on the outer septagon.

Coercion is used through implied or direct threat generating fear. Referent power relies on using a charismatic personality, much as Ronald Reagan did when he was president of the USA. Expert power uses persuasion. Having information gives the holder choices denied those without the information. Legitimate power relies on the formal rules of the organisation, my position as your manager is backed up by regulation to reinforce my position. Reward power is used exchanging what you have for what is needed by the person over whom you are exercising power. Connection power makes it in their interest to do as you ask; consider the connection power of the boss's secretary.

When considering power it is important to use the most appropriate power base for the situation. Use of coercion with knowledgeable and experienced project team members is probably not a good idea. Exchanging knowledge is more likely to be successful. Legitimate power is difficult to use on cross-functional projects where staff may not recognise the power of another department manager. In the brochure project most of the team work for other departments so you would use reward, connection or expert power depending on the situation.

Power and perception

The determinant of whether a power can be used does not rest with project managers, it rests with those over whom the project managers are trying to exercise power. If they are not perceived as having a particular power, then they will be unable to use it effectively.

For example, imagine that you have had a nice meal in a restaurant with your partner and the bill came to £90. To your horror you have left all means of paying behind but you have £1000 in your account at the bank. You approach the restaurant manager, explain your predicament and ask if you can go home and return with your cheque book. The restaurant manager will look you up and down and if you are untidy, dirty and drunk, then your watch and driving licence or passport will be needed as security before you leave. If you are polite, respectable, clean and sober, you may be permitted to leave and return without further ado.

The fact that you have £1000 in your current account will not help you unless the restaurant manager *perceives* that you have the money. So it is with your people: you must use the power bases they perceive and not those you yourself think you have.

Leadership style

Tied to your use of power is your preference as to style of leadership. Using an appropriate leadership style is of particular importance when you have a project team of mixed experience and ability. On your brochure project you have Jill Guido who is both experienced and committed. Fred Mayes is reasonably competent but is a bit variable in commitment and Jim Franz is very keen but does not yet know much about the work he is being ask to do. Leading them all in the same way is likely to be counter productive for two of the three. Your choice of leadership style is impacted by three main factors:

■ Task
■ People
■ Situation.

Let's take each in turn.

Task

If you have done before what you are being asked to do now, your style will be rather different from doing a completely new task. If the task is relatively easy, you will apply a different leadership style to that for a task you consider difficult. Thus the task itself will impact your chosen style of leadership.

People

Your leadership style will also be impacted by the 'tools' that you are given to work with. If you have experienced capable people who are keen to carry out the project, then your style will be different from dealing with new starters or those unfamiliar with project working.

Situation

How much time, money and resources have you been given? How confident are you that you can do this well? How are projects done in this organisation (the culture)? The situation will again impact your leadership style.

These three areas are very much situational inasmuch as your choice of leadership style can vary considerably depending on the overall situation in which you find yourself. So which styles are available to you and how do you choose which one is suitable for a situation?

The approach to leadership taken by Hershey and Blanchard is particularly useful to project managers as it recognises many conditions that are experienced in projects. The very nature of projects tell you that there has to be a beginning, a middle and an end. As you move through a project, the situation changes and with it leadership priorities. You have staff of varying competence and commitment and you will be using a number of power bases to lead them. All this recognises that projects are delivered in a number of circumstances or *situations*. Hershey and Blanchard explored 'Situational Leadership' which recognised that leadership styles should adapt to changing circumstances. This asks you to consider how you behave when leading your people considering both *task behaviour* and *relationship behaviour*. Behaviour in this context means the outcome of a combination of your personality and the situation in which you find yourself.

Personality + Situation = Behaviour

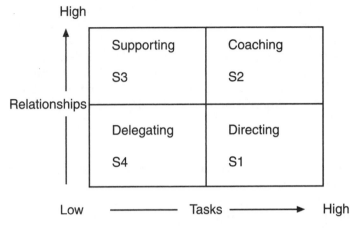

High

Relationships

| Supporting

S3 | Coaching

S2 |
| Delegating

S4 | Directing

S1 |

Low ——————— Tasks ——————▶ High

Figure 12.2   One structure

If the situation changes then the behaviour will likely change.

Task behaviour concentrates first on getting the project activities done. Meetings will be about planning and coordination of tasks and meeting deadlines and so on.

Relationship behaviour is about spending time with the project team and its members. Giving them coaching, counselling and support in their work and being available and open to them. This goes back once more to motivation. From the two behaviours comes one structure (Figure 12.2). Here four leadership styles emerge. Let's look at each of them.

S1

Has a high task and a low relationship focus—is a *Directing* style of leadership, telling people what to do. This style is appropriate when working with team members of low maturity. In other words they have high commitment but are low in competence. This is the first level maturity, or M1. Staff joining a project are all M1 because although they may have a great deal of expertise about the technicalities of the project they have not done *this* project before so in the early stages they need to be told what to do. The decisions are made by the project manager and staff implement them.

S2

Has both a high task and a high relationship focus—is a *Coaching* style of leadership, which motivates team members to carry out the project manager's decisions. This style fits best when team members have a low commitment and a variable competence. This is a level two stage of maturity—M2. This stage may occur once the project is under way and a setback on a task has 'switched off' a team member. Or early expectations of working on the project do not match the realities. In these events the project manager works with the team member concerned to set objectives for them and then coach them to achievement of those objectives; but the decision is still made by the coach for the team member.

S3

Has a high relationship and low task focus—is a *Supporting* style of leadership which asks team members to make their own decisions but strongly supported by the project manager in the reaching of that decision. You use this style most effectively when you are dealing with team members who may be feeling variable in commitment but are high in competence. This is the third level of maturity—M3. This style will be needed if there is rework of a repetitive nature to be done or if there is a change of project specification which means that some work already done becomes irrelevant. None of us likes to see efforts wasted and if they are, then commitment to the project could drop. Or you may be asking people to work on tasks they do not particularly enjoy. In this case the project manager using S3 will encourage the team member to set new objectives and will support them in the defining of these objectives and in their implementation. It is important that the project manager leaves the team member to make decisions using their own high competence. Decisions made by the team member are more likely to be implemented than those made for the team member by the project manager. If the project manager insists on making the decisions then S2 coaching is being used.

S4

Has a low relationship and low task focus—is described as a *Delegating* style of leadership. Use this style when you are in the fortunate position of having people who are both highly committed and highly competent—the fourth level of maturity—M4. Here you are working with staff who know what they are doing and who are also keen and willing to get on with the project. In these circumstances you should leave them to get on with it without interference.

There is a questionnaire which allows individuals to report their preferred leadership styles whether S1, S2, S3 or S4. Having used this questionnaire for many years with project managers I find that the overwhelming concentration is on S2 and S3 styles of leadership. S1 and S4 lag well behind.

S1 is avoided because mature leaders can see the Directing style of leadership as an 'immature' style. But when people are new, regardless of their expertise, they need guidance, someone needs to tell them how things are done. They look to the project manager for guidance, leadership and instruction. S1 is also appropriate at the end of a project when you are driving for the finish. Your project staff will know of their next assignment or they may already be involved in other projects, so you must focus them to drive for the finish line.

Project managers like to be in control and this can prevent delegation or the use of S4 style of leadership. Delegation means the handing over of an important part of the project by taking risk, in hoping that someone else will do an important task well. It is not about getting another to do the boring bits that you don't want to do yourself. Delegation motivates and advantage should be taken of an opportunity of freeing yourself up for other work. Delegation is not popular on projects for many reasons; such as the wish to lead from the front. Or you may not be seen as having done the work if someone else does it—and they might get all the credit for a job well done. If you stay in this frame of mind you will be unavailable to do other work and you will not be seen as capable of developing a successor.

The links between power, maturity and leadership style can be summarised (Figure 12.3).

When deciding which leadership style to use first carefully determine the maturity level of the person you are working with. From there choose the leadership style and then the power bases that are suitable for that style.

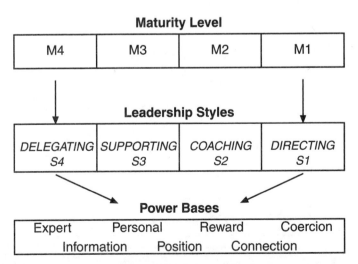

Figure 12.3   Matching power, leadership style and maturity

Now go back to Jill Guido and the brochure project and start with maturity (M). She is committed and competent (M4) and is therefore to be led using S4 or delegation. *But do not delegate before she has settled in to the project* and understands fully what needs to be done and you can see that she is plainly confident. Initially use S1 and S2; thereafter, use expert power to exchange views and opinions on how things should be done and in due course delegate.

Jim Franz is keen but does not yet know much (M1). Therefore, it would be appropriate to use S1 and S2 from the beginning and perhaps all the way through the project so reward, connection and coercion powers might be used.

Fred Mayes can be a bit variable, somewhere between M2 and M3. Therefore, in general, make decisions for him using S2 or he can be supported in making his own decisions using S3. Use a mix of personal, positional and reward powers. Should he ultimately show willing and display competence then you might delegate to him.

As you start projects you will be setting objectives for your people and directing them about the project and how it is to be done. As progress is made and you move to the peak of activity (Figure 12.4) apply a leadership style to match the needs of each individual which means using all four styles. As you drive for the end of the project when schedule features highly, you will find yourself coaching and directing those remaining on the project. Please note well that this is a generalisa-

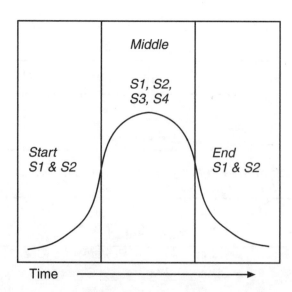

Figure 12.4   Leadership style and the project life cycle

tion and that each person needs addressing as an individual, to understand their maturity and from there the leadership style that suits them.

If you can identify the appropriate style for each of your team members you have a useful motivational tool. The use of an inappropriate leadership style can do much to de-motivate team members.

Motivating individuals

In understanding how to motivate people when working on projects you should know the factors that help motivate. Where people are not working directly for you, as in the case of the brochure, motivation can prove a difficult subject. It can be felt that because you have little formal authority over them there is little you can do to motivate directly. This is not the case. There is much misconception about the nature of motivation and mistakes can be made from these misconceptions.

We know from the work of Herzberg and Maslow that there is a difference between those things that satisfy or dissatisfy and true motivators (Figure 12.5). For example, money is often considered a motivator

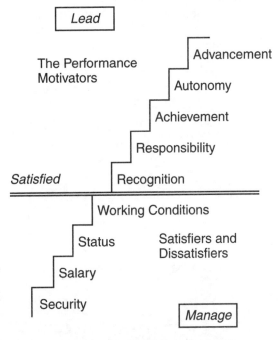

Figure 12.5   Motivation balance

when in fact it has more to do with satisfaction or dissatisfaction. If you are not paid enough, then you will feel dissatisfied and you may be demotivated. However, if you are well paid, you will feel satisfied but not necessarily motivated. Think about your last big pay rise; it may have motivated you for a month or two but by the third month it had become the norm. Bonuses may motivate but look at how the bonus was spent to gauge the true motivation. Often bonuses motivate because they indicate achievement and recognition. Looking at Figure 12.5, 'satisfiers' can be seen below the line and true motivators above the line.

Poor working conditions will dissatisfy but putting them right will only remove the dissatisfaction, it will not necessarily motivate unless people feel that they are also being recognised.

It should be understood that even if all the factors that cause dissatisfaction are present, it does not mean that to motivate is impossible—it is just harder to do. For example, volunteer workers in famine or war-torn countries have dreadful working conditions, no salary to speak of, their security is zero, their very lives are in danger and they enjoy little status, yet they are often the most highly motivated people. They are motivated by personal achievement through taking responsibility and the recognition they receive from those they are trying to help.

Project managers are seldom able to influence the context of the organisation in which they work, unless they are senior. The context is typically to do with the satisfiers which surround the job content itself (Figure 12.6).

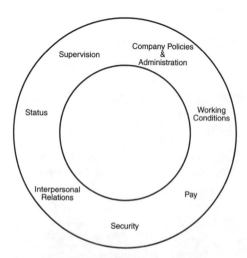

Figure 12.6   Job context

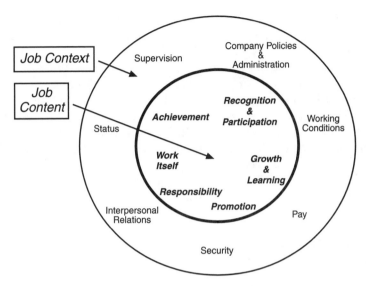

Figure 12.7   Context and content of the job

As project managers you may not be able to do much about the policies and procedures of your organisation, so the best you can do is to reduce dissatisfaction by getting your people motivated above these issues.

To motivate your people you have at your disposal the real motivators that live inside the job content—these are the tools that you use to lead the motivation of your teams.

When considering leadership and in particular motivation, describe the satisfiers as being the *context* of the work you are doing and the motivators as defining the *content* of the job (Figure 12.7).

Practical motivational tools

To motivate your people make them feel valued. It is essential that they are well briefed and up to date with progress on the project as well as their own progress. They should feel involved and accepted as an important contributor to the project and team.

Recognise individuals by praising them and communicating that praise to other team members during meetings or in project bulletins.

Train your people to use their new skills so that they see their own growth and learning. Team members can also train each other to help build relationships and teamwork.

Provide challenge by increasing individual responsibility. Foster ideas from individuals and give them the responsibility for carrying them out. Identify and train a deputy to take over as project manager should it be required.

Each of us is different and this applies to motivation. What motivates me will not necessarily motivate you. Knowing each of your people as individuals is the only way to be sure that you are using the correct tool to motivate. Individuals often do not know what motivates them because they have never been asked to think about the subject, so asking may not produce the right answer. Observation and spending time with team members will throw some light onto what it is that people like to do. If you can match the needs of the project with the needs of the individual then you will have achieved motivation.

Disclosure

When trying to discover what motivates your team members you should be aware that you are seeking privileged information which will not be given lightly. The conversation that takes place must be sensitive or the true individual motivators will never emerge. When you seek to grow relationships with your people you move gradually from safe areas of discussion to more risk-loaded discussion.

There are five levels of disclosure (Figure 12.8). They happen in sequence and you must respect each level.

Level 1—Ritual and cliché

When meeting someone for the first time you apply Ritual and Cliché. In the UK you say 'How do you do?' And the only response expected in return is a 'How do you do?' You do not expect to hear about a headache or a backache—it is not the right answer to the ritual.

Level 2—Facts and information

When a conversation starts, it will remain on a level of exchanges of Facts and Information. How many children? Where do you live? What do you do? And so on. There may be no progress beyond that level. But if there is further disclosure then you will move to Thoughts and Judgements.

Level 3—Thoughts and judgements

Now you will express opinions about relatively safe areas, nothing too

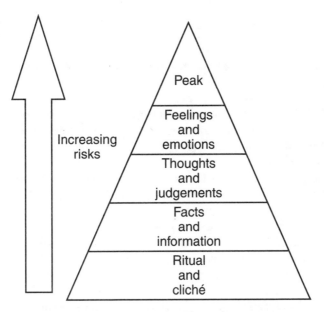

Figure 12.8   Five levels of disclosure

personal and nothing too challenging or threatening but nevertheless more risk is being taken in being open. If all goes well and a relationship is forming then you can climb the triangle together.

Level 4—Feelings and emotions

You begin to open up to express true Feelings and Emotions about particular situations. This is where you might find out about the real agendas that are operating within individuals. Of course, if you are open about feelings and emotions, then you will be more likely to elicit an open response. It all depends on the level of trust that can be grown. It can take hours to reach this level and sometimes it will take years. We hear of long-married couples who have lost the ability to communicate with each other, so they no longer express true feelings and emotions.

Level 5—Peak

In Western culture there are not many working relationships that reach peak—when you know everything about the other person. In working terms this may not always be a comfortable place to be. You may be told about intentions to seek employment elsewhere which can draw you into conflict between loyalty to the person and loyalty to the organisation. It needs careful handling.

The point to remember about this disclosure triangle is that you have to make progress upwards. If you miss a level out then you are likely to find yourself remaining in ritual and cliché even though you are seeking feelings and emotions. The other person will either tell you nothing or what they think you want to hear; both amount to the same thing. You must give your project staff time to make their way up the triangle at their own pace if you want to grow open relationships.

It is important that you know what motivates each of your people; when you do you can lead them better and you will have the means by which you can persuade them. For example, if you know that Fred Mayes likes cricket you might give him an afternoon off to watch England play if he does a particularly nice piece of work. If you know that Jill Guido likes to travel away from the office occasionally, you can ask her to go and visit the photographer to check progress. Jim Franz enjoys golf so an early afternoon off can be traded against some catch up work during an evening. At peak, individual personal hopes and aspirations for the future can emerge.

This is highly motivational stuff but remember that if this information is disclosed to you, it must be kept confidential and acknowledged in some way. Expectations will have been raised and it is your duty as project leader to do something about meeting these motivations. If a team member hopes for promotion as some future stage then you are obliged to develop this person through training and delegation. Ignoring the information is de-motivational as the person will feel that having taken the risk of disclosing something personal, they are not now being taken seriously.

Reaction to change

Individuals implementing projects frequently become de-motivated by too much change. Unless you have perfect foresight you are unlikely to produce a plan that will be delivered in its entirety; it will change during implementation. Change does not necessarily demoralise, it is often how change is delivered that causes problems. Change follows a predictable path and acquaintance of this path is most useful to project managers whose projects are invariably about change of one kind or another. I have yet to hear of a project definition which asks for the *status quo* to be maintained. This predictable path is known as the change curve or the transition curve (Figure 12.9).

In the transition curve there are two axes, the *x* is time and the *y* is the individual's perceived competence to deal with the change—how

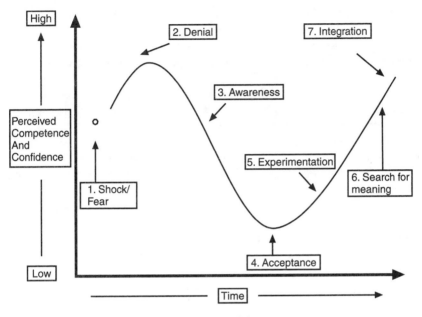

Figure 12.9   Transition curve

confident they feel about embracing the change. To help understanding you might like to recall a significant change in your own life—a new job, a huge lottery win or more likely and depressingly a death or a divorce or some other major change. You pass through seven major stages *en route* to integrating a major change.

Stage one—Shock

If the change came out of nowhere then you will feel shock which renders you incapable of any action except panic and immobilisation. This shock is reduced if prior warnings have been given but this is not always possible.

Stage two—Denial

In this second stage, your perceived ability to cope with the change rises. This is because you use the coping mechanism of denial. You have decided that this change is not actually happening. You cope by burying your head in the sand in the hope that the change will go away. You can observe this happening even in the most positive of changes when people winning large sums of money insist that they will continue working and that they will not move house—they are denying that this change will affect their lives. Denial is seen on projects when work not needed is still being done by an individual who has personally invested a great deal of time in the task.

I remember working with a colleague who had spent three weeks producing a complex proposal for work in Kuwait. It took up the time of two administrators. As it neared completion President Saddam of Iraq invaded Kuwait and the Gulf War started. I had a need for urgent administrative help, so on that morning I asked one of the administrators to help me as the Kuwait proposal was going nowhere for the time being. When my colleague arrived at work later that morning he was furious about what I had done. No reasoning with him could help, he had done the work, he wanted it finished. I had to relent so as not to totally undermine him with other staff. He had gone strongly into denial and would not be moved.

Stage three—Awareness

Here confidence starts to slip as it is realised that the change will happen. Re-work, change specification, whatever it is, is going to happen. There may be minimalisation which accepts that change is happening, but there will be low cooperation and limited acceptance. Anger and frustration are common at this stage.

Stage four—Acceptance

You are now feeling at your least able to cope, but the good news is that the change process is well under way. You are accepting now that the change has happened and that it will impact you. You are fed up but the re-work is just going to have to get done or it is unimaginable that that person will not be around any more. The pain here can be great but there can also be resignation. You can now build a platform for the world after change.

Stage five—Experimentation

You will try out a couple of things to see what the change will do, you experiment. You start making new friends, or to do things in a different way. You may stop sulking if that has been your response so far.

Stage six—Search for meaning

You try to understand what the change means for you. You may now look at the past and recognise that things could not stay the same and that may be this change is not so desperate after all. This re-worked task is producing a better result than the original. My new friend has many improvements over my old friend.

Step seven—Integration

The change has happened, the pain, if not forgotten, has lessened and can be lived with. It is now hard to remember how things were before and performance is likely to improve.

As human beings we are all in a number of transitions at any one time, both at home and at work. We are also in different stages in those transitions. We like to change at our own pace and we accept some changes more readily than others. So it is in your projects. When you institute needed change, you cannot expect all your people to 'zip' through the transition curve immediately. Indeed, you should be wary of those who appear to accept major change without batting an eyelid—it is unlikely that they have, especially if the change was not forewarned. Those people who may be the fiercest resistors, given time to progress through the curve, could end up your fiercest allies once they have integrated the change. Those who 'zipped' through could be outside sharpening knives and eyeing your shoulder blades. Give people time to accept change on projects and you will find them easier to motivate through the change process.

Now that you understand a little more about leadership and the motivation of team members on projects let's move on in the next chapter to the leadership of teams.

References

P. Hersey and K.H. Blanchard (1977) *Management of Organisational Behaviour: Utilising Human Resources*, 3rd edn, Prentice-Hall: Englewood Cliffs, N.J.

F.J. Herzberg (1959) *The Motivation to Work*, Wiley, New York.

D. McGregor (1960) *The Human Side of Enterprise*, McGraw Hill, New York.

A. Maslow (1954) *Motivation & Personality*, Harper & Row, New York.

Building and leading a project team

Management, above everything else, is about people. It is about the accomplishment of ends and aims by the efforts of groups of people working together.
John Harvey-Jones *Managing to Survive*

People approach us in only two ways, as individuals and in groups—or teams.

Teams are unique. They are comprised of different people doing different things and therefore have a 'personality' of their own. In today's working environment we are likely to be members of several teams at once and we will feel differently about each of them. Teams are complex affairs with as much going on beneath the surface as above. They are not just groups of people trying to do something.

For the purposes of project management my own definition of a team is 'A group of people with a high degree of interdependence, working towards the achievement of a common task.' The key word is *interdependence*. Individuals cannot achieve their own objective by themselves, so reliance on others is a major contributor to teamwork. For example, a soccer team is a team because no one player, however brilliant, can put the ball in the back of the opposition's net unassisted. However, an international golf or tennis team may find it difficult to produce good team behaviour as each of the individual members has a primary goal of personal success. It is the accumulation of individual success that produces team success, so therefore the primary focus will be on self success. It is quite possible to build teams without interdependence, it is just harder to do.

Project teams are generally teams or sub-groups of teams producing tasks. We can find teamwork on a project as a whole, but more likely we will find teamwork on the task activities themselves. The project manager must bear in mind that each member of the team will have their own agenda about the project and their personal success may be different from project success. For example, a team member may be unwilling to work faster simply to bring the whole project back on track. He was given two weeks and two weeks he'll take. This is where the project manager needs to lift the needs of the project above the needs of the individuals. This can be done by growing a project team so that mutual support and commitment to the project as a whole is forthcoming.

Project managers need to understand what happens in teams and how best to achieve teamwork. This chapter will cover how teams develop and what roles we all play when in teams and how we can use them. There is a process for a first team meeting in the hope of getting off to a good start followed by a summary of what we should be doing during the stages of the project life cycle.

Getting commitment from teams

It is seldom that teams get together and just 'click'. A work group will follow a defined sequence that is predictable. When looking at growing the commitment of your project team, it is essential to take this predictable sequence into consideration. The sequence is about behaviour, how each of us behaves in a team situation, how we react and feel about others in a team. Much of our behaviour is subliminal, learned from our days playing and reacting with other children in the nursery and subsequently through schools and into work. If we can make ourselves conscious of what happens in team situations then we can recognise what is happening and manage the process of team building better. Developing a project team has five separate stages.

Stage 1. Forming

This occurs whenever a prospective team meets for the first time. People are polite, watchful and guarded and may not present their true 'selves'. During this stage they are weighing up the other people in the group and are looking for how they might fit into the team. Typically they will have a good deal of dependence on the leader and will look to the leader for structure in the meeting. The role of the task leader at this stage is to ensure that everyone is included and that clear direction is given to the group. This is the 'forming' stage.

Stage 2. Storming

When the group starts to get down to the business at hand it will move to the storming phase. This phase involves a degree of conflict and can be noisy. Much testing of relationships takes place as we look for those who share our views and attitudes and conversely for those who would do things differently. We also have expectations about the roles we might play in the team and we can find a mismatch between our expectation and the actuality when someone else takes the role that we chose for ourselves. Again this is a behavioural process which will happen within any developing team. At this stage groups often describe them-selves as being 'stuck', complaining about not getting anywhere and this is all rather a waste of time. They may already be disillusioned with the leader for allowing this stormy situation to develop. It is the role of the project manager to ensure that the storming process does not get out of hand. He or she must focus on the task. Polarisation and sub-grouping within the team must be avoided and cooperation encouraged. However, remember that the team is following a well understood process as it moves towards development.

Stage 3. Norming

Emerging from the storming phase, there is better understanding each of another. The group starts to use its own language and tolerance of differences will be more readily accepted although discussions can remain robust. The leader can start to delegate responsibility to the team and a less 'hands on' approach can be used. Conflicts should be dealt with immediately and a constant focus on task delivery main-tained. There may be residual storming behaviour continuing into this phase.

Stage 4. Performing

This is a rather nice place to be with a team. The team has reached synergy and is performing to a level previously considered unlikely. But there is great team cohesion to the exclusion of outside individuals. This team thinks it can achieve anything and frequently does! The issue for the team leader here is to ensure that the work does not suffer whilst the team enjoys itself. There also may be a degree of 'groupthink' when team members will not debate problems vigorously because they are trying to avoid conflict which might move the team off its 'high'.

Stage 5. Transforming

This stage is particular to project teams. By definition, projects must finish at some point. As completion nears, the project team disperses and starts to move on to other things. During this time the task leader must drive for completion. Too often, things are allowed to slip at the end when the task is practically delivered. Ensure that individuals meet their objectives fully; they are probably thinking about their next task rather than dealing with the fiddly, unimportant end bits of their current project. For example, I had some beautiful work done by a particularly skilled carpenter. But all my wife remembers is that he didn't clear up properly when he had finished. If we are doing the office move—who is going to take away the empty crates as soon as they are finished with? If we are producing the brochure how will we ensure that the distribution process takes copies to the desk or hand of those expecting them? Most of us will have experienced the installation of a piece of software on our computers which came complete with inadequate training or manuals.

These five are known as the Stages of Team Development. If we reach the Norming or Performing stage and someone leaves or joins the team, then we go right *back to the Forming stage*. This is particularly important for project managers. When an activity is being done by three people and it gets behind, it is too simplistic to assume that putting another person on to the team will always speed things up. It often achieves just the opposite as a Norming team goes back to Forming to accommodate the new arrival. These stages are concerned with relationships, so if there is a change to the team, the relationships within the team will alter. If you are in a team at the moment and you do not recognise the Storming phase then most probably your team has not gone through it. This does not mean that the team cannot carry out its objective—it can and will but not with the ease and commitment of the performing team. Rupert Eales-White in his book *Creating Growth from Change* (McGraw Hill, 1994) describes what it feels like to be inside a team at each of the four primary stages:

- Forming: confusion
- Storming: conflict
- Norming: cooperation
- Performing: commitment.

It is in your interest to move as far along the stages of development as early as possible to benefit from the advantages of teamwork on your project.

Another important factor is to consider your own and others' behaviour when working in teams. If you are permitted to behave in your own preferred ways, then you are likely to enjoy the team and the project. If for some reason you are not permitted to behave in the way you want, you will find dissatisfaction with the team and may cease to contribute fully.

For example, I attended a development course as a participant which included people from many parts of the world. Early in the programme we were put into groups of six to carry out an exercise. Other members of my group came from various businesses, most being at middle management level. There was also a university lecturer who was about thirty years of age. When the exercise began, the lecturer intervened and immediately started to tell us all how the exercise was to be done. He was quickly but politely challenged by more than one other person until agreement was reached to follow an alternative plan. The lecturer was visibly stunned and in quite some pain. That evening in the bar I was able to speak with him over a drink and in due course I asked him how he felt about what had happened. It became clear that he was used to directing teams of students carrying out projects and he had assumed that this was the role he would adopt in the lecture room team. On trying to adopt that role, during what was the storming phase of a new team containing rather more experienced members than his student teams, he felt strongly rebuffed. Although he didn't physically withdraw he most certainly mentally withdrew whilst he sorted out what had happened to him and what he should do next.

Team roles

What he experienced was a conflict of Team Roles. Team Roles were presented by Meredith Belbin (*Management Teams: Why They Succeed or Fail* (Butterworth-Heinemann, 1981)) after he observed a large number of teams over a ten year period, operating on a business simulation. You can use his work most usefully in project management, as Belbin identified eight distinct roles that are played out by people when working in teams. These eight are described below.

Coordinator

They coordinate efforts and get all project team members involved. They look for individual strengths and ways to apply them to the project.

Shaper

Extroverted and dominant, the shaper will enjoy leading activities if given the chance but they can fall into conflict with other shapers.

Plant

Introverted ideas person. Belbin said all successful teams have at least one strong plant. Very sensitive to criticism about their ideas, they are concerned with the big picture. Detail is not their strong point.

Monitor evaluator

Analytical and logical. They will focus on facts and present them as such. They will not be swayed by empty excuses or promises of jam tomorrow. They will analyse the situation but may be harsh in judgement and therefore are sometimes seen as insensitive to the feelings of other people.

Team builder

Holds the team together. Give them the project team outings to plan and deliver, they will persuade everyone to come and enjoy doing so. Relationships are all important and as a result they can be indecisive, preferring to remain neutral rather than deciding in favour of one course of action over another.

Resource investigator

Extroverted and resourceful ideas person. They tend to have a large network of contacts and are good at bringing outside support into a team.

Finisher

Worries about details and chases people up. The finisher will look after the completion of tasks and activities ensuring that they are aware of where the project is in relation to the bar chart. They will enjoy digging down into the detail for facts.

All of us are a mix of these team roles and we use every role at some time or another during the implementation of a project. The ease with which one style over another is used is purely a matter of preference. It is not about ability. For example, I know I have a very low preference for finishing but I must finish all the time to get my work done; but left to my own devices and desires I would rather do something else. I may not enjoy finishing but it does not mean that I am not perfectly good at it.

Applying team roles

To apply team roles look at *some* of the activities that are required to be carried out with project teams. These will include:

- Organising
- Directing
- Generating ideas
- Team cohesion and morale
- Analysing and focusing
- Details and deadlines.

Organising

You need to be organised to ensure that the work of the team as a whole contributes to the successful completion of the project. A degree of social skills is important to ensure that each member feels a part of the team and is able to contribute. This activity is provided by the co-ordinator. In projects this would most likely be done by the project manager to steer the team in the direction wanted using available strengths in the team.

Directing

The project team needs direction, ensuring that each team member knows the why, what and how of the project. Clear instructions need to be given and drive instilled to get the work done on time and at the right cost and quality. Again, these activities are likely to be carried out by the project manager for the project as a whole. This is directing activity and is the comfort zone of the shaper. Shapers are easy to spot—they like to be in charge. They are dominant and out going and sometimes a little noisy. They challenge and debate but can be offended if the team doesn't accept their choice of action. They are action-oriented and not given to introverted thinking. They will enjoy shaping tasks as part of the project.

Generating ideas

Ideas are essential for problem solving as well as for identifying best routes forward. Ideas are particularly important as projects, by their very nature, have not been done before. Therefore, project work is a great environment for trying out new ways and new approaches.

Ideas come from two of the roles in the team—the plant and the resource investigator.

The plant is highly creative but introverted. They need to be drawn out and encouraged; their ideas are often half-formed but valuable; the great danger for the project manager is to allow criticism of a half-formed idea from a plant. Left-brained organisations and people will do this but logic and analysis can be strongly negative when applied at the wrong point of the creative process. A criticised plant withdraws further into introversion keeping all further ideas to themselves. The project loses out. In leading a plant, ensure that there are only 'good' or 'interesting' ideas but never bad ones. Ideas build upon each other so one may look odd but together with another half-idea may be of enormous contribution.

The resource investigator is the extroverted ideas person. They love to network and pull resources into the project, even acting as a 'Mr Fix-it'. They are outgoing, fond of the latest idea but a bit short on follow through. Finishing anything is not a strong point unless deadlines demand action. They like to be liked, so are diplomatic and good with customers—particularly in the selling role.

Team cohesion and morale

The project working environment can be a pressure cooker, full of tension and stresses, especially when things are not going to plan and the team is working flat out in difficult circumstances. Personal relationships can become strained and if left unchecked can develop into damaging friction and at worst deliberate interference to prevent others' success.

Enter the team builder. Team builders promote harmony in the team. They are sociable and personally non-competitive. They can be good at translation—telling one team member why another is behaving in a particular way. And they are supportive of all team members personally striving to keep the team unified and morale high. Because of their harmonious bent, they are not always good decision-makers.

Analysing and focusing

You want to know what is going on in your projects, how they are progressing against plan and so on. You would also like to know exactly where the variations are and what is driving these variations. The project needs to be focused ensuring that it is not diverted part-way through by some interesting but irrelevant blind alley. You are looked after here by the monitor evaluator. Intelligent, analytical and pointed.

They can see through situations and may deliver the fact bluntly and without guile or art. This can make them appear cold and aloof. They are essential to a project team provided that they are kept on a positive bent and work with some degree of tolerance of others. On identifying a monitor evaluator the updating of control charts can be delegated to them. They will enjoy the work and the delegated responsibility and may give insight when reading the results.

Details and deadlines

Successful projects meet their deadlines. Meeting the project deadline is a result of meeting many smaller deadlines and milestones set for all the activities and tasks. 'Drift' on these activities and tasks will see the project overtime. Encapsulated in meeting deadlines is attention to detail; on projects the devil can be in the detail. Here you must rely on the proclivities of the finisher. They worry about details and will check what they are told. They chase people ensuring that they do what they said they would. These are the people who track you down on holiday. 'You said you would do it—now where is it?' Of course, this can make them rather unpopular but if they keep your project to schedule this may have to be tolerated. Great in project teams.

Team roles mix

On reading the above descriptions you may recognise yourself in more than one team role. We are all a mix of team roles, and so have the ability to move between them. In the project team each team role needs to be fulfilled. Identifying individual project member preferences can be done by asking team members what they would like to do to contribute to the project. Most will volunteer for those activities that have most appeal for them. Any essential activities left over will have to be given out equally.

The key points to remember about team roles is, first, to allow your team members, as far as make sense, to adopt the tasks which lets them use their preferred team roles. And, secondly, to cover all the functions of the roles.

Having understood that project teams follow a pattern of development and that individuals in project teams have preferences about what they do in a team you can move on to a pragmatic process for getting your project team off to a good start at the beginning of a project.

Team building

The first step in team building is getting off to a good start. Of course, team building is a subject of its own and not all steps can be listed here; but those discussed below are steps you can take to increase the chances of success.

Meet

Get everybody together. With luck and planning you will personally have met everyone or at least had telephone conversations with them. This first meeting should be before the task is under way and reasonably informal but still focused. Invite those who may not be needed for some time, otherwise when they do join, existing members will plummet back to the forming stage. This may happen anyway but at least the face will be known by team members.

Step 1: Introduce

Ask each member to introduce themselves, choosing a more confident member to go first to set the right tone. Even if they know each other it is worth doing as the eye contact and listening to each other helps the forming stage. If necessary give them a structure to follow, such as:

- preferred name—what you like to be called;
- what you do for your organisation;
- what you did before you joined this organisation;
- something about yourself, hobbies, family, something you are particularly proud of;
- what you want to get out of doing this task;
- any concerns that you have at this stage.

Stage 2: Brief

Move on to give an outline brief of the project—even if you have given it to most of the people in the room, once is not enough. Use the structure developed in Chapter 2 to ensure that they fully understand where the project came from and what it will do to solve the issue addressed. If you have a flip chart there is nothing wrong with making the process transparent, so have the model (Figure 13.1) drawn ready or re-build it starting with the *Why?* And then working round anti-clockwise.

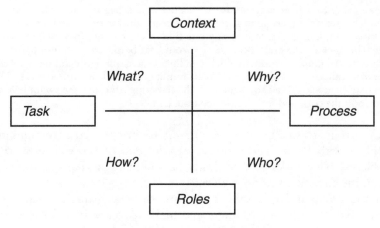

Figure 13.1   Briefing model

Take questions and be careful to note and give full consideration to any suggestions. Involve the quieter members and try to dampen the over-enthusiastic. The briefing is important but the meeting of each of the team is equally so.

Step 3: Team activity

Carry out an activity in which the team can share. You might like to stay within the task in the hope of generating ideas and solutions and to get people talking to each other. The activity should be a part of the task that has a solution or else the meeting could break up with a feeling of failure, something to be avoided. Encourage creative thinking about the problem and ask people to generate a quantity of solutions building on other offers. Don't allow criticism of ideas at this stage—that comes later; for now they should freewheel to explore possibilities and suspend judgement. When ideas are exhausted, group them into categories and see if there is anything usable. There always is!

Alternatively, give the team an exercise to do that has nothing to do with the task but is fun and helps draw people together. I frequently use exercises to stimulate the creative juices (something all enjoy) and to encourage people to let their hair down and move away from the forming stage. I have a whole library to use—my children enjoy them too. For example, a variation of the fox, the duck, the corn, a river and a boat.

A man came to a river carrying a fox, a duck and a bag of corn. There was a small ferry tethered by rope to a jetty but he could only carry himself and one of the three with him in the boat at any one time. He could not leave the fox with either the duck or the grain because she would eat both. He could not leave the duck with the grain because the duck would eat the grain. How did he cross the river with all intact? (Give them 15–20 minutes to work it out. Answer: The man tied the duck behind the boat with the tethering rope and she swam behind as he took the corn and fox over in separate trips!)

If the group is small, ask each person to bring a creative thinking problem with them. The problem can be one of those investigative problem-solving tasks that can only be solved by asking questions to which the answer yes or no is given.

If the group is large, split it up into rotating teams so that each person works with all the others and make it competitive for a minor reward.

Step 4: Team mix

Look at the mix of the team. You will have an idea of the practical skills and experience from their track record but what about the roles they prefer when working in teams?

You saw earlier that teams go through stages of development. Progressing from stage-to-stage depends on the state of the relationships between the team members. Those relationships are often determined by the happiness or otherwise of members. How content the members are depends upon how satisfied they are with the role they are playing in the team. If a member likes to produce the ideas for the team—is he or she being allowed to do so, or is someone else doing all the creative stuff? Is there a member who prefers to give direction rather than receive it, who is not being permitted to give directions? There may be a content individual who revels in detail work, looking after the network diagram and reporting on progress for instance.

Being permitted to use preferred team roles is helpful to the overall effectiveness of the team. You can find out much more during one-to-one meetings by simply asking members what they like to do when working in teams. With some prompting you can identify preferred team roles.

It may be felt that all this is rather unnecessary and contributes little to the task. But in fact it is time very well invested indeed. If you can forge strong relationships within your project teams you will gain the benefits of a performing team sooner in the project. This process takes but a few hours and results in the team being well forward of where they would be by concentrating solely on task.

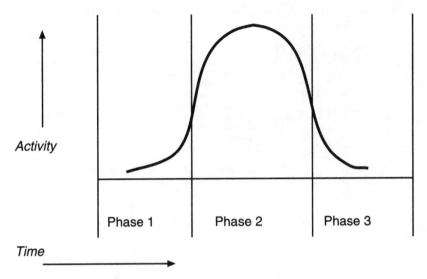

Figure 13.2   Life cycle of a project

Team leadership and the project life cycle

You saw earlier that projects have a life cycle (Figure 13.2). The life cycle has three overlapping phases, a beginning, a middle and an end. Phase 1 looks at the feasibility and the definition. Phase 2 deals with the planning and the implementation of the task. The peak of the work is during this phase when most people are employed on the task. Phase 3 sees the hand over of the completed project and any updates for the future.

When looking at teams the life cycle becomes important when considering maximising the benefits from a performing team. Most project teams start work in the hope that teamwork will emerge. If it does it happens in phase 2. If it doesn't it is still phase 2 and the busiest part of the work, it is too late to be thinking about building teams now. Teams need to be built in phase 1 to allow maximum benefit during the whole project delivery. Therefore plan to do it and spend time planning it.

For each of the three phases there are actions that project managers carry out to give the best chance of building a performing team. They are summarised in the following figures.

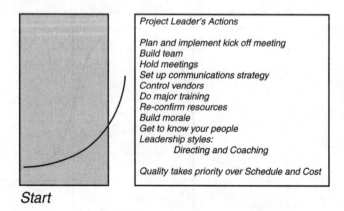

Figure 13.3   Beginning the project implementation cycle

Summary of leadership activities

Phase 1—beginning

Phase 1 is when project success is set up (Figure 13.3). Omitting any one of these activities will have consequences for the project further down the line. It is an expensive phase but any worthwhile investment is expensive when setting up, when everything goes in but little comes out.

Phase 2—middle

Phase 2 should be seen as an opportunity to reduce the pressure on the project manager after the initial setting up phase. It is time to use all the leadership styles (S1–S4) and to look for motivational activity for individuals and the team (Figure 13.4). Delegation and team responsibility will free us up to do other things.

Phase 3—end

Success in building a performing team allows a drive for the finish line. The team will have robust relationships and will readily cope with extra reasonable pressure. There will be regret in the team as the project

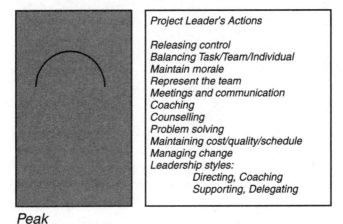

Peak

Figure 13.4   Middle of the project implementation cycle

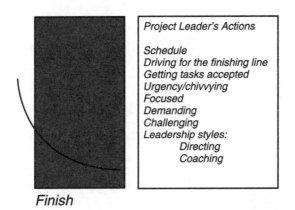

Finish

Figure 13.5   End of the project implementation cycle

completes but when you ask for volunteers for the next project they will walk towards you. Time for the project end party.

The previous two chapters have introduced the subject of people both as individuals and as teams. The motivation of people is the most challenging activity for any project manager but in many ways it is the least understood and the one most open to luck in delivery. It is hoped that these chapters have given some insight about what can go wrong in the leadership of people on projects along with some helpful techniques about how to improve success rates.

Solving implementation problems

To solve a problem it is necessary to think. It is necessary to think even to decide which facts to collect.
Robert Maynard Hutchins

Project implementation is a complex and tricky business. It needs all the skills of the experienced manager, from sound understanding of project definition through to the patience of Job when handling the project team. It is difficult to deliver a project to meet all its objectives whilst keeping it under control and not experience problems along the way. On projects, even 'small' problems will always occur.

This chapter addresses a structured approach to problem solving. Project problems are no different from other business problems and if a structured approach is used then much progress can be made. Here is such an approach and a demonstration of how it can be used.

Step 1: Accept that a problem exists and resolve to take action
It may seem rather obvious but remember that the start of a problem is the introduction of a change or transition. Things are not about to remain the same. In Chapter 12 the transition curve showed that after unwelcome change has been announced most people go into denial—denying that the change is actually happening. This is what happens on projects if care is not taken. So the first thing to be done is to acknowledge that a problem exists. There is a difference between what is expected, the desired result, and the actual result.

When running simulated projects in the lecture room it is astonishing how many teams of experienced managers watch unattractive trends grow weekly on their control charts and do nothing about them. These teams live in hope that next week, as if by magic, this trend will recover all by itself. Be a monitor-evaluator and look dispassionately at what is going on. In these situations blissful ignorance is often preferable to knowing the truth but for those project managers intent on doing a good job such an attitude will not help. Blissful ignorance does come with a comfort factor but it is not the real world and is therefore unsustainable. Project managers must dig and delve to understand what is happening on projects.

Step 2: Dispassionately gather the facts
When gathering data about a problem it has to be done dispassionately.

As facts are collected it is too easy to leap to conclusions and make inappropriate decisions. This cuts off the process and information further in the gathering process could change a point of view. It is easy to be led down blind alleys or to go off chasing red herrings because of emotional involvement. Success or failure might depend on this. However, it is best to remain dispassionate and continue gathering information.

Problems encountered in project work are more often a combination of a number of things and it is a trap to go casting around looking for the one right answer that will put all right. Complexity means that there is more than a single factor contributing to the problem. Dealing only with one of the factors involved can end up in dealing with symptoms instead of causes. For example, imagine a man fixing a car tyre who is frantically pumping it up to get back behind the steering wheel and on his way as fast as he can. He hasn't lifted his head from the task at hand to see that the road in front is covered with the shards of broken glass that caused his original problem and that as soon as he moves his car, he will have at least one more flat tyre. Without dealing with the real underlying problem by sweeping away the glass, he will achieve very little other than a repeat of the original problem. In these circumstances stop, think and apply a problem-solving analysis tool to ensure that the dynamics of the problem is understood.

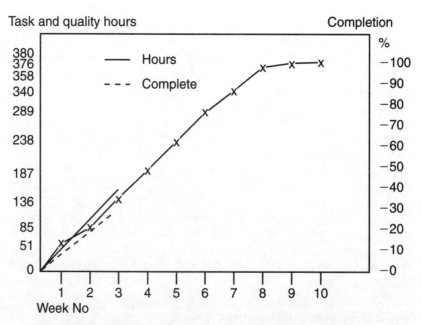

Figure 14.1   Task hours and percentage complete (week 3)

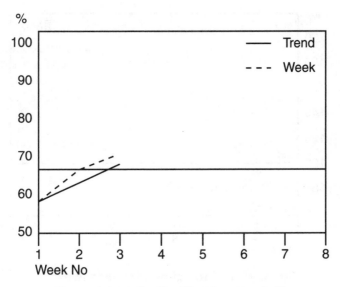

Figure 14.2   Staff utilisation (week 3)

First, gather information—what is known? This process can be illustrated using the brochure project problem started in Chapter 11.
Remember from reading the controls there is a gap developing in task
hours and percentage complete chart for week 3 (Figure 14.1). The
solution to the problem in terms of what had to be done was identified
but what caused the gap in the first place was not explored. By blindly
continuing there is no reason why the problems that caused the gap
should not impact equally the future.

So what is known? Some tasks are behind even though the required
hours and more are being spent. Too many hours are going in and too
little is coming out in the form of project completion. The staff utilisation chart (Figure 14.2) has more data.

The trend is pushing above the target base line and the weekly report
is already well above. This confirms the previous chart. Team members
are working hard but not necessarily effectively. This points in the
direction of performance, the effort is being put in but the performance
appears to be low (Figure 14.3).

Although our project performance is on a rising trend it is still well
below the plan. There is a definite problem here that is impacting the
project and it needs to be addressed.

Step 3: Define the problem

Having identified that there is a problem and that it needs to be dealt

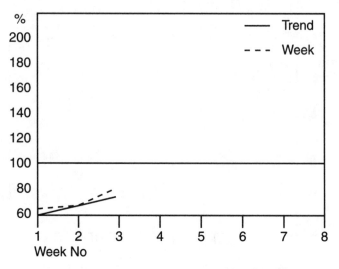

Figure 14.3   Project performance (week 3)

with, it needs to be defined and understood. But again there are factors that interfere with a good problem analysis.

As we make our way up the greasy poles of our careers we start off with simple problems that often have a single right answer. We find it quickly, solve the problem and we feel good about our performance. However, when we are leading projects we are facing many more problems of a complex variety, the easy ones are solved by staff on the tasks themselves. If we apply the same process to complex problems as we use for simple problems we will come unstuck. When we are dealing with simple problems we look for the one right answer; the single issue that is causing this problem that when removed will make all the problems disappear. With projects sometimes there is a single issue to blame but far more likely there is a number of factors contributing to a more complex problem.

Generally, as human beings we like our problems to be simple so we look to simplify problems so that we can apply simple solutions. This leads to inappropriate problem solving resulting in fast but incorrect decisions being made which in turn cause their own problems, until the project manager is totally confused about what decisions caused which effect. At this stage the project is out of control.

From the facts dispassionately gathered it is known that the team are working too hard for too little, the performance is way down on what was expected so there is a 'performance gap'. Our project machine is being given the raw material but it is not producing what it should, producing too much wastage in the process. The problem is defined but what is causing it is not yet known.

Step 4: Understand what is causing the problem

Again the temptation here is to jump to conclusions. 'We knew that Fred Mayes would be a problem and I'll bet he isn't cooperating with Jill Guido.' Looking for the single right answer—the solution to all the problems is common. It doesn't work and must be guarded against. Analysing is a left brain, emotionally detached process. There is nothing wrong with using gut instinct but it should be checked and confirmed using fact.

The problem has been expressed as one of performance. What impacts project performance? To explore this use a fish bone or herring bone technique to break down performance into its component parts. This is a problem-solving method that gives a visual representation of the areas that could be contributing to a problem. To do this list down all the factors you can think of that impacts project performance. Use the Herrmann example built for project implementation (Figure 14.4).

There are left brain task factors to consider and there are right brain process factors to consider. Select those that might be impacting project performance and add them and any others to a fish bone diagram (Figure 14.5).

Then look at each factor in turn and investigate fully where they are in the project. Check thoroughly and ensure that the right checks and balances exist for say the allocation of overtime on the project. Check that the right people are working on the tasks that they enjoy. Check that there is control of the critical path and that tasks are not being held

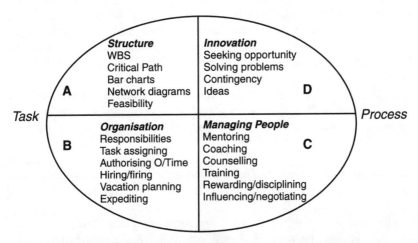

Figure 14.4   Project implementation: example of Herrmann

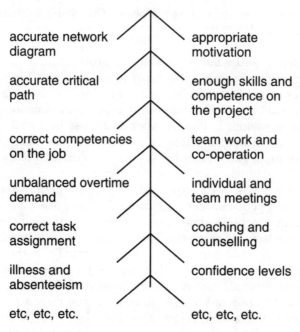

accurate network
diagram

appropriate
motivation

accurate critical
path

enough skills and
competence on
the project

correct competencies
on the job

team work and
co-operation

unbalanced overtime
demand

individual and
team meetings

correct task
assignment

coaching and
counselling

illness and
absenteeism

confidence levels

etc, etc, etc.

etc, etc, etc.

Figure 14.5   Performance fish bone

up unnecessarily, and so on. However, looking back at the staff utilisation control chart. The project is well above the target line of 65 per
cent for the last week and the trend is firmly upwards. Going over the
target line means taking hours away from somewhere else. Utilisation is
up but performance is down and note that 65 per cent of project hours
were allocated for task and the remainder for activities to support the
project; leadership, motivation, training, meeting, coaching and so on.
So it is from these areas that the extra time must be being taken, so
there could be a right brain problem. So build a second fish bone
diagram (Figure 14.6).

Again, look at each element and thoroughly check each to ensure that
it is being done. Typically with a performance problem, project managers turn off the leadership and motivational factors of the project.
Leadership and motivation are acts of faith and when the project falls
behind it is all too easy to steal the hours from what is perceived as
'non-productive' activities. This may be what is happening here. As the
hours are added to utilisation so they are being taken away from performance factors (Figure 14.7).

Therefore be doubly sure that meetings are being held, both with
individuals and the team and that scheduled leadership activities are
being carried out as planned. During this analysis, options for action

Poor skills   Wrong competencies on task

Poor plan   Too many interruptions

People leaving   Tasks not clear

People joining   No communication

Moving people   Too much overtime
from task to task   being taken

Team friction   Inadequate briefing

etc, etc, etc.   etc, etc, etc.

Figure 14.6   Performance and people factors

will emerge. There will be a selection and discarding of options as each contributing factor is analysed in turn but do resist the temptation to discard any options without checking first.

At this point, there is nothing wrong with asking the members of the project team what they think is going wrong. Care has to be taken as the feedback can point in all directions, especially if it is a stream of consciousness without much structure.

A simple questionnaire can be used to help structure and focus feedback; it can be completed anonymously if it will help openness and honesty. A questionnaire is helpful in drawing out many areas of discontent in a team. The results should be presented back using team

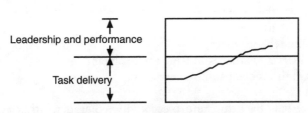

Leadership and performance

Task delivery

Figure 14.7   Staff utilisation

averages only preferably in open discussion at a team meeting. Draw up your own questionnaire (Figure 14.8) using a progressive scale, scoring from 1 to 6 prevents a middle score allowing people to sit on the fence. Start it off with a question.

Average the results so that each person's report is kept confidential. The feedback from the team survey will give a useful contribution to identifying which factors from Figures 14.5 and 14.6 need addressing. Completion of these questions can draw out common perceptions of strength and weakness of the team. As project manager you start with the strengths, pointing out the achievements in that area and thanking people for their efforts. This will help a free and open exchange about the weaker areas. Ask for concrete examples of undesirable behaviour and encourage team members not to be over defensive whilst trying to grapple with the underlying causes of problems. Distinctions need to be drawn between dislike and necessity. For example, not many people actively like meetings and even the most effective and well run meetings can be poorly reported. This is a matter of judgement; however, common complaints need investigating. Continue discussions until there is some clarity about the factors needing change. The more specific the nature of the change needed, the more easily correct action can be taken.

Step 5: Plan the change and implement it

Having decided to take action it needs an implementation plan. It is important to try and identify which of the options will bring the most change for the least effort. Trying to change too many factors at once will hide which actions are producing which effects. Knowing which decisions produced which results means being properly in control of the project.

Summary

In summary, when faced with a project that is not running according to plan and there is uncertainty about the cause, that is the time to switch on a problem-solving process.

Step 1 Accept that a problem exists and resolve to take action
Step 2 Dispassionately gather the facts
Step 3 Define the problem
Step 4 Understand what is causing the problem
Step 5 Plan the change and implement it

From here it is back to the project and keeping a weather eye on the control charts to gauge the results of decisions.

Keeping this particular project in mind, how would you rate the presence of the following factors in this Project Team?

	True		Sometimes True		Not True	
1. Tasks are on time	1	2	3	4	5	6
2. Utilisation is climbing	1	2	3	4	5	6
3. Quality is climbing	1	2	3	4	5	6
4. There is commitment to the successful delivery of the project	1	2	3	4	5	6
5. Team members offer ideas to the project	1	2	3	4	5	6
6. Customer complaints are falling	1	2	3	4	5	6
7. There is no conflict between project team members	1	2	3	4	5	6
8. The project manager gives direction and guidance	1	2	3	4	5	6
9. The team does meet often enough	1	2	3	4	5	6
10. Everyone contributes to team meetings	1	2	3	4	5	6
11. People are satisfied with project team meetings	1	2	3	4	5	6
12. Project status reporting is only concerned with numbers	1	2	3	4	5	6
13. Project team members trust each other	1	2	3	4	5	6
14. I feel appreciated for doing good work	1	2	3	4	5	6
15. I am clear about the purpose of the project	1	2	3	4	5	6
16. I always know what I should be doing on my tasks	1	2	3	4	5	6
17. I feel supported on the project	1	2	3	4	5	6
18. I am involved in decision making that affects me or my work	1	2	3	4	5	6
19. I am free to take action in my tasks without reference upwards	1	2	3	4	5	6
20. I do not get blamed unfairly when things go wrong with my work	1	2	3	4	5	6

Figure 14.8   Questionnaire

Glossary

Project management has a language of its own and some of the shorthand used can be complex and confusing for the uninitiated. Here some of the terms more commonly used in project management are defined. They should supply what you need for most projects at work.

Project	A distinct piece of work which has a specific time limit, defined by objectives and is unique in that it has not been done before.
Task	A quantity of work which is part of a project having its own specific deliverables, costs, resources, and time limit.
WBS	Work Breakdown Structure. A means of organising a project into logical, understandable tasks by breaking down work into smaller and smaller manageable packages. Ultimately a package will typically be no longer than three weeks of work and no shorter than one week.
Predecessor task	A task that must be completed before the next dependent task can start. A task may have more than one predecessor.
Successor task	A task that cannot begin until the previous task has been fully completed.
Typical hours	An estimate of the hours of effort needed to perform a task.
Duration	The time required to complete a task.
Network diagram	A flowchart which represents the project, showing the relationships between tasks.
Forward pass	A forward pass goes forward through a network diagram producing the earliest dates that tasks can start and finish.
Backward pass	A backward pass comes backwards through a network diagram producing the latest start and finish dates for a task.
Early start	The earliest time a task can begin.
Late start	The latest time a task can begin without delaying the project.

Planned start	The time a task is expected to begin.
Actual start	The time a task actually begins.
Early finish	The earliest time a task can be completed.
Late finish	The latest time a task can be completed without delaying the project.
Planned finish	The time the task is expected to be complete.
Actual finish	The time a task is actually complete.
Slack	The spare time available for a task to be completed on schedule.
Critical path	The longest route through a network diagram which gives the project's overall duration.
Critical task	A task on the critical path which must be completed on time if the project is not to be delayed. These tasks will have no slack available to them.
Bar or Gantt chart	A graphic display of project tasks which shows how they are related to each other in time.

Index

Bold type indicates a principal reference
Italic type indicates a reference to the glossary

absenteeism 102
absorbing extra work 35
acceptance of change 162, 163
acknowledging problems 181, 188
activity data summary 34–5
activity description sheet 33
Adair, John 54, 117, 147
added value 91
agendas
  of individuals 159, 165
  for presentations 108–12
appendices to written submissions
  109
assertiveness 112

backward pass calculation 38–9, *191*
bar charts 44–6, 51, *192*
behaviour
  determinants of 150–51, 166
  when working in teams 168–9
best practice 103
'big picture' thinking 20
Blanchard, K.H. 150
BMW 82
'bracketing' 35
breaking down of tasks *see* work
  breakdown structure
briefing
  on particular tasks 71, 101
  on the project as a whole 174–5
budgeting 97–105, 145
  coherence in 97
  'finger in the air' approach 98
business case for a project 20

CD-ROMs 69
change curve *see* transition curve
change, reactions to 160–63
clarity in defining a project 18–20
coaching 69, 101
coaching style of leadership 151–2
'cockpit chart' 135–6
coercion 147–8

coherence in planning and budgeting
  97, 107
cohesion of a team 172
commitment 15, 56, 123, 165
communication 57
competencies 61–2
  assessment of 62–3
computer packages *see* software
conclusion of a project, approach to
  153–4, 167
confidence in a project 44, 56
connection power 148
context 20, 157
contingency plans 74, 77–80
contracts *see* employment contracts;
  psychological contract
control charts 129–42
controls and control systems 99,
  125–8
  use of 136–45
'coordinator' role 169
costing 94–5, 105
  of meetings 101
creative thinking 176
crisis management 14
critical path 39–41, 77, *192*
critical task *192*
customer relationships 89–90, 102,
  134
customer satisfaction 81, 86–8,
  134–5, 140–41
cutting costs 105

data gathering 181–2, 188
deadlines 173
decision-makers, presentations to *see*
  presentations
Defensible Plan, components of 8,
  13–14
definition
  of a problem 183–4, 188
  of a project 17–26, 144
delegation 152–4

delighting the customer 81–4, 90–93
    passim, 134
    cost of 94–5
    as distinct from satisfying 86–8
denial 161–2, 181
directing activity 171
directing style of leadership 151
disclosure, level of 158–60
distance learning 68–9
duration of a task *191*

Eales-White, Rupert 168
early warning signals 74, 77, 79, 133
earned value 136–9, 142
effort needed to complete a project
    100, 129, 133
emotional needs and responses 88,
    119, 121, **159**
enhancements **90–91**, 92–5
    cost of 94, 98–9
    identification of 134
estimation of time needed 35
executive summaries 109
expectations
    discrepancies between 86
    raised by disclosure 160
experimentation 162

favouritism 57
feedback 56
feelings 121, 159
final hours, forecast of 133, 139–41
'finisher' role 170, 173
finishing time *192*
    working back from 39
    see also conclusion of a project
fish bone diagrams 185–7
fitting together the parts of a project
    35–6
'flat' organizations 2
float *see* slack
forming–storming–norming–
    performing–transforming
    sequence 166–8
forward pass calculation 36–8, *191*
fox–duck–corn–river–boat problem
    175–6

Gantt charts 44–5; *see also* bar charts
graphics 51
groupthink 167

Harvey-Jones, John 165
helpers with projects
    initial recruitment of 31–2
    later involvement of 41
    see also technical support

Herrmann, Ned 119–22, 185
Hershey, P. and Blanchard, K.H.
    150
Herzberg, F.J. 155
hierarchical organisation 5
human resources planning 49

ideas and 'ideas people' 170, 171–2
impact/probability matrix 76–80
implementation cycle 66–7
    beginning, middle and end of
    178–9
implementation plans **60**, 145
    elaboration of 63–72, 93–5,
    100–101, 188
    'holes' in 102
    risks in 74
    work breakdown of 118
implementation of projects, overview
    of 117–23
incentives 56
individual meetings *see* one-to-one
    meetings
individual motivation 155–7
individual needs of team members
    54–7, 69, 117–18, 122, **147**
information: historical, diagnostic and
    prognostic 128; *see also* data
    gathering
initiators of projects **18–19**, 26, 92
insurance against risk 77
interdependence of team members
    165
internal customers 81, 84
introduction of team members 174
involvement of team members and
    other helpers 41, 56

job content
    and context 157
    and satisfaction 156
'just in time' training 68

labels for activities 33
leadership 53–72, 117, 122–3, 144
    absence of 118, 186
    planning for 72
    power bases of **147**, 153
leadership activities, summary of
    178–9
leadership style 149–55:
    influences on choice of 150
    in relation to life cycle of project
    154, 177
learning curve 59
'left brain' thinking 119
levelling of a project 45, 47–8, 144

life cycle of a project 7–8
  and leadership style 154, 177
listening 56
logical structuring of tasks 28
logical thinking 120–22, 172

McKinsey, J.O. 13
Maslow, A. 155
matrix working 5–6
maturity of team members, levels of
  151–3
meetings
  cost of 101
  see also one-to-one meetings;
    review meetings; team meetings
'monitor-evaluator' role 169, 172,
  181
morale 172
motivation 56, 58, 117, 122
  as distinct from satisfaction 155–6
  of individuals 155–7
  promotion of 157–60, 178–9, 186
need
  for a plan 14–15
  for a project 18–20
  three spheres of 54–6, 58, 61,
    117–18
needs of team members see individual
  needs
network diagrams 35–41, 44–6,
  50–51, 191
  transformed into bar charts 46
'norming' stage of team development
  167

objectives
  of a project 19, 56
  of training 68
on-the-job training 68–9
one-to-one meetings with team
  members 56, 70, 101–2, 186
one-to-one presentations to decision-
  makers 108
operational management 3–4, 6, 17
organising a team 171
organisational competencies 61
organisational culture 26, 150
outsourcing 84

peaks of activity 45
percentage complete 132–3, 138,
  143, 145, 182
performance control 129–30
performance gap 184
performance percentage 138–9
'performing' stage of team
  development 167

personal attributes 64–6, 70, 78–80
personal preferences 61, 176
persuasion 107, 110
plans, need for 14–15; see also
  written plans
'plant' role within a team 169, 172
'political' dimensions of a project 23,
  26
power
  perceptions of 149
  relationship to influence 147–8
  relationship to style of leadership
    and maturity of team members
    153
predecessor tasks 34–5, 191
presentations 107–13, 145
  conclusion of 113
  time needed for 111–12
priorities, setting of 98
proactive approach to risk 77
probabilities, assessment of 75–6
problem solving, structured approach
  to 181–8
process shortfall 58
process thinking 22, 121
profile of resources 45, 47
prognostic information 128–9
'project', definition of 191
project management, nature and
  importance of 3–4, 6–7, 17
project performance chart 129–30,
  139, 184
project planning
  'how' of 21–2
  nature of 15
  outcomes from 16, 18, 34
project reviews 91–2, 102
project status table 137
psychological contract 85–6, 88, 134

quality, measurement of 90
quality hours 99–101, 132
quality planning 83–5
quality procedures and quality process
  88
quality reviews 92, 145
questionnaires for probem-solving
  187–9
questions at presentations 112

Reagan, Ronald 148
recognition 156, 157
relationship behaviour 150–51
resentment 58
'resource investigator' role 169, 172
resource allocation of 60–61, 63–6
resource requirements 43–51

responsibility, allocation of   158
review meetings   91–2
rewards   56, 148
rework   102
'right first time'   83
risk
    associated with disclosure   159
    associated with planning   15
    management of   73–80, 145
roles of team members see team roles

satisfaction, levels of
    of customers   86–8
    of team members   155–7
scheduling   27–41, 144
self-study   68–9
'shaper' role   169, 171
situational leadership   150
skills
    'capture' of   59–60
    opportunities to use   32, 56
    technical   49
slack   39–40, 192
    free   49–50
    taking up of   45
Smith, Adam   81
social events   70, 101–2
software
    for learning about project
        management   69
    for undertaking project
        management   27, 50–51
'spare' time   38
specifiers of projects see initiators
sponsors of projects   18–19
staff planning   44–5
staff utilisation chart   130–31,
        139–40, 183, 187; see also
        utilisation percentage
stakeholders   22, 84
standards of quality   88, 99
standing project teams   59–60
starting time   191–2
status forecast   143–4; see also
        project status table
'storming' stage of team development
        166–7
stress   14, 41, 103–4, 145
successor task   191
supplier reviews   92, 93
supporting style of leadership   152
surprises at meetings with senior
        managers   110
synergy   58, 167

task
    definition of term   165, 191

focus on   22, 54–6, 61, 117–18,
        121, 123
task behaviour   150–51
task briefings   71, 101
task hours   99–101
    charting of   132, 138, 143, 145, 182
task reviews   91, 93
team activity   53–8, 175
'team builder' role   169, 172
team building   58, 67, 69, 174–6
team competencies   63
team development, stages in   166–8
team maintenance   54–8, 66, 69,
        117–18
team meetings   56, 58, 70, 101, 186
team mix   176
team roles   23, 26, 169–73, 176
    personal preferences for   176
technical support   49
templates for project plans   16
thanks   113
Thatcher, Margaret   55–6
thinking style   22–23, 119–23
time, unallocated   102
time allocated
    for motivating people   56
    for particular activities   32, 35, 45
    for planning generally   16
    for presentations to decision makers
        111–12
    for sequences of activities   36–8
    for team meetings   58, 67, 71
    for training and coaching   67, 69,
        71
training   66–70, 101, 157
    methods of   68–9
    of team members by one another   69,
        157
'transforming' stage of team
        development   167
transition curve   160–61, 163, 181
trends   125
typical hours   191

utilisation percentage   103–4

vague instructions and objectives   18
validity of control measures   129
values   57
visualising a project   28

'what if' process   142–5
'whole-brained' decisions   123
work breakdown structure (WBS)
        28–30, 111–12, 117–18
written plans   13
written submissions   108–9, 113,
        191